To: Cynthia Naatehn-Gobh,
Much Success in your
Professional endeavour!!!.

(signature) , 7/22/12

Liberia: America's
Footprint in Africa

Liberia: America's Footprint in Africa

Making the Cultural, Social, and Political Connections

JESSE N. MONGRUE, M. Ed

iUniverse, Inc.
Bloomington

Liberia: America's Footprint in Africa
Making the Cultural, Social, and Political Connections

iUniverse books may be ordered through booksellers or by contacting:

iUniverse
1663 Liberty Drive
Bloomington, IN 47403
www.iuniverse.com
1-800-Authors (1-800-288-4677)

ISBN: 978-1-4620-2164-2 (sc)
ISBN: 978-1-4620-2166-6 (hc)
ISBN: 978-1-4620-2165-9 (ebk)

Library of Congress Control Number: 2011909946

Printed in the United States of America

iUniverse rev. date: 02/14/2012

Dedication

THIS BOOK IS DEDICATED TO MY WIFE,
AUDREY DUNDAS MONGRUE AND OUR FOUR
CHILDREN: REMCY, TIFFANY, WONSER AND
LAYAMON FOR THEIR LOVE AND SUPPORT.
I WOULD ALSO LIKE TO DEDICATE THIS
ACCOMPLISHMENT TO MY LATE SON, CHUKUKA
WHOSE UNTIMELY DEATH WAS CAUSED BY A
HOUSE FIRE IN QUEENS, NEW YORK CITY IN
2000; FROM WHOM THE INSPIRATION CAME TO
WRITE THIS BOOK.

CONTENTS

LIBERIA: AMERICA'S FOOTPRINT IN AFRICA ASPIRES TO BE A TEXTBOOK, PERHAPS MORE FOR AMERICANS, BECAUSE OF THE LIMITED INFORMATION AVAILABLE ABOUT UNITED STATES AND LIBERIA'S CULTURAL, SOCIAL, AND POLITICAL CONNECTIONS. THE AUTHOR HAS ALSO PRODUCED FOR THE GENERAL PUBLIC AN ACCOUNT OF AMERICA'S ROLE IN THE FOUNDING OF THE LIBERIAN STATE AND HOW AMERICAN EXAMPLES HAVE MARKED DEVELOPMENT OF THE AFRICAN STATE OF LIBERIA FROM ITS NINETEENTH CENTURY INCEPTION TO THE PRESENT.

DR. ELWOOD DUNN
PROFESSOR OF POLITICAL SCIENCE
UNIVERSITY OF THE SOUTH
SEWANEE, TN 37383

THERE IS A LOT OF TRUTH TO THE SAYING, "THERE IS NO PLACE LIKE HOME." THERE IS THE TENDENCY, HOWEVER, THAT THE LONGING FOR ONE'S HOME DISSIPATES INTO OBLIVION WHEN ONE HAS BEEN IN A DIASPORA FOR A PROLONGED PERIOD OF TIME. JESSE MONGRUE HAS CHRONICLED A BOOK THAT NOT ONLY IGNITES A STRONG FEELING OF PATRIOTISM, BUT ALSO PROVIDES AN INSIGHTFUL HISTORY OF LIBERIA AND ITS RELATIONS WITH THE UNITED STATES OF AMERICA. THIS BOOK RECEIVES MY HIGHEST RECOMMENDATION FOR PRIVATE AND ACADEMIC READING.

REV. DR. FRANCIS TABLA
PASTOR OF EBENEZER COMMUNITY CHURCH,
BROOKLYN PARK, MN 55428

Acknowledgments

For the development of this book, my thanks and appreciation go to the following people: Mr. Joe Lavein, a Liberian entrepreneur whose insightful council contributed to the development of my work; Susan Hintz, former superintendent of Osseo Area Schools (ISD 279) for her support and advice that led me in the right direction; Joseph Johnson, former associate professor at the University of Liberia for offering me some critical analysis early in the process; Miamen Wopea, a Liberian educator, for providing some insights toward this document; Troy Anderson, technology integration specialist at Osseo School District for periodically providing me technical assistance whenever there was a need in that area; Samuel Annor, an electrical engineer who lives in the Twin Cities of Minneapolis/Saint Paul; Ernest Norris, a graphic designer (also from the Twin Cities), for providing additional technical support; Steve Smarjesse, former instructor of language arts and world language and now a full-time professor at North Hennepin Community College; and Rev. Dr. Francis Tabla, pastor of Ebenezer Community Church, who was instrumental in the presentation of my work in the community.

I owe a great deal of gratitude to Mr. Ijoma Flemister, former member of the House of Representatives, Republic of Liberia, and now a professor at Ohio State University; Dr. Patricia Jabbeh Wesley, a Liberian poet and professor of English at Pennsylvania State University; and Dr. Elwood Dunn, a professor of political science at the University of the South at Sewanee, Tennessee, for giving me scholarly advice. All of these esteemed colleagues are unique authorities on Liberian history. I gathered wisdom from their empirical and longitudinal research on the topic. Their advice was helpful toward the development of my idea. I am grateful also to Ms. Amy Cutler, managing editor of Beaver's Pond Press of Edina, Minnesota, for providing me with technical support toward the development of this book.

The success in the development of this book is also the result of interviews with many mentors, advisors, and elders in the Liberian community, friends who invested their time, energy, and interests in my cause. I am extremely indebted to all my professional partners, both Americans and Africans, whose perspectives gave me the motivation to continue my writing. I benefited immensely from their comments, advice, and critiques in developing this book. For all of their contributions to my work, I am exceptionally grateful. I also owe any measure of success of my work to the array of input from so many ordinary people whom I met at different social gatherings, church functions, and so on, some of whom do not wish to be mentioned in this book. Without these tremendous sources of motivation and encouragement, this work would not have been possible.

Foreword

What would the fate of America's automobile industry be during World War II without Firestone Rubber in Liberia, the World largest rubber plantation? Would American military advantage over German position in the war in North Africa be possible without Roberts Field, an airbase built in Liberia as a springboard for transatlantic movement of US troops and logistics to avoid sinking of US war ships over North Atlantic by the Germans? In this book, the author has also produced for the reader a historical account of America's involvement in the creation of an African state of Liberia for free American blacks who wanted to return to Africa during the early part of the nineteenth century. The author has chronicled an account that depicts the cultural and social connections between African Americans and Americo-Liberians (free American blacks) who immigrated to Liberia in the early part of the nineteen century.

As an African American, reading this book created a personal connection for me both culturally and socially because of the similarities the text produced between these two groups. Few of these cultural and social connections between African Americans and Amerco-Liberians are the use of Ebonics in America, a term referred to the language of all people descended from enslaved black Americans, particularly in West Africa where the nation of Liberia is located; you will also note from reading this book that ten Liberian presidents were born in the United States, one born in Barbados, the Caribbean; and another born in Freetown, Sierra Leone; making a total of twelve Liberian presidents who were born outside of the country. And the appreciation of Western values such as the names (especially last names), religious practices, fraternal practices, and how the two groups engage in social activities. I had the opportunity to meet with the author, and I found him to be an avid reader of US/ Liberia's relations who has done extensive research on the cultural, social, and political connections between Liberia and the United States. He is also an educator and a historian who has spent a number of years studying relationships between the United States and Liberia.

What is great about this book is the chronological order established by the author, making it an easy-to-read book. It clearly informs readers which events precedes the next; for example, in the first few chapters, the author produced an account that led to the creation of the American Colonization Society, (the philanthropy organization that sponsored the African colony on the West coast of Africa) known today as Liberia. Not only is the book written to inform but to educate the general public especially American audience a unique point of view by the author in narrative forms, of the historicity for those free American blacks who decided to emigrate to the land of their ancestors. The book contains vital insights about the social dynamic of the Liberian society. Whatever you do, don't miss chapter nine called "The Liberian Outlook," talking about the composition of various ethnic groups in Liberia and their way of life. It alone is worth the price of the book. You will get a clearer picture of the Liberian people.

To all prospective readers, you will be reading a book that has been empirically and longitudinally researched by the author to offer a well balanced assessment of the relationships between Liberia and the United States of America. It also matters for me to write this foreword because this is truly a cross-cultural document that has been produced for both Liberian and American societies. Finally, and most important of all, from reading this book you will be informed about the role of America in the founding of the Liberian state and relationships between two nations that have lasted 195 years.

Lester R Collins
Executive Director
State of Minnesota
Council on Black Minnesotans

Preface

Dear Reader:

You will be reading this book during an era of post-Cold War relations between the United States and Liberia, a period when Liberia has made history in producing Africa's first female head of state. You will also be reading at the beginning of a relationship based on "mutual respect," the core principle of America's first black president, Barack Obama's, foreign policy. In short, I invite you to read this book with objectivity and an open mind, but at the same time, to celebrate the more than 180 years of history between the United States and Liberia. To my primary audience—students, educators, and other professionals—I encourage you to study it, understand it, and evaluate it. This book is a historical document written to serve as a source of information to those who are interested in learning *why* and *how* Liberia was founded.

Another reason for writing this book is to inform the general public; especially American audience about a very important history that most people are unaware of. This unique and essential account has not been objectively told as it should be—for the benefit of all—but more importantly, for the younger generation who know very little or nothing about the history between the United States and the Republic of Liberia. There is a generation of children born in the United States with Liberian parents who have very little knowledge about the country their parents came from. They have a right to understand the culture and social dynamics of the people who helped to establish this little West African nation, Liberia's similarities to the United States, and the role of the American Colonization Society in its establishment.

Before going into the historical context of the relationships between these two interrelated countries, let me begin with a story of a young man who grew up in the countryside of Liberia, a little town in northeastern

Liberia at a time when there was no road to link it to a public highway, no running water, and no electricity. School was occasionally closed due to a lack of teachers, so going to school was interrupted for most, except for the lucky few who managed to live in or travel to big cities where basic resources such as schools and hospitals were readily available. In an environment like this, one has to be extremely grateful to any parents who would let their children leave home for some distant city to attend school, especially when the parents knew no relatives in those cities. I was that young man who managed (with the blessing of my parents, especially my mother) to leave a town with limited resources to get an education. Most of my childhood friends were not as fortunate as I was to leave.

It was with such determination to get a better future for myself that I came to the United States twenty-five years ago. Writing this book is my way of giving back to the community and society at large. In a true sense, I am giving back to Liberia, a country that I am a product of by birth. Coming from such a humble beginning, making it to the United States, and soon to be an author is a blessing. There is nowhere in the world that my story could have even been possible but in America.

I am an educator and a policy analyst—or more simply, student of politics—but I also love history. For several years, I have done research on Liberian history and African Americans. Some of my studies have been about the contributions of African Americans in the United States and in Liberia, which I have presented in workshops to educators, community leaders, parents, students, and teachers.

As educator, my primary job is to inform, but public policy plays a major role in the development of my analysis. As in everything we do, politics is the method by which people live together; it is the method by which we decide how to meet our basic needs, solve common problems, and protect ourselves against threats, both foreign and domestic. Moreover, it is through politics that we seek to realize the good of life for ourselves and our communities. In a broader sense, this book was written not just as a historical retelling of the United States and Liberia, but to examine why decisions are made and how those decisions affect people for many generations. One chapter is devoted to why decisions are made and another chapter addresses how those decisions influenced the initiatives that led to the creation of Liberia.

This book is the result of a three-year empirical and longitudinal research work conducted on US/Liberian relations. Ideas that contributed to the creation of my work also came from reading literary works by Liberian and American educators and by interviewing community leaders and historians with knowledge of the topic. Many scholars have written research papers, perhaps, an article or commentary about specific issue; so I thought it would be wise to produce a book for the general public or for academic use. I also wanted to leave a legacy, and one way to do that is by producing a document that would continue to inform and educate people long after I am gone.

To my primary audience, the expectation is that this book will serve as a conduit between the peoples of two great cultures. By reading this book, I hope people will have a different perspective about both countries and their relationship, and ultimately, about the African continent in general. I am ever mindful that not everyone who reads this book will agree with the content or all of the issues addressed; however, I encourage my audience to keep an open mind about the information contained herein. I trust that something will make sense.

I therefore invite you to take a great voyage of discovery of those events that led to the creation of an American colony that eventually became the Republic of Liberia. You will also discover the major players in the decisions, their primary goals, and what the consequences of those decisions (good or bad) were afterward. I welcome you to relax, enjoy, and read with an intention to be informed. I also ask that you please serve as a conduit or liaison as you seek to understand the cultural, social, and political connections between the United States and Liberia.

—Jesse Mongrue, M.Ed
Liberian Historian & Educator
Saint Paul/Minneapolis, Minnesota, 2011

Introduction

Did you know that more than a hundred thousand African Americans emigrated to Liberia before and after slavery ended in the United States?

What have you been told about the social, cultural, and political connections between United States and Liberia?

The title of this book—*Liberia: America's Footprint in Africa*—was given to argue the story that people have always believed that Liberia is a country that was founded *for* freeborn African Americans, not by them, as is widely believed. There is a history between the United States and Liberia that needs to be told for the younger generations. While it is true that some free American blacks attempted to achieve this goal of establishing a country in Africa, their efforts were limited by a lack of funds or moral support from some in the African American community as evidence by the Philadelphia meeting of African American leaders who opposed the idea of going back to Africa.

There have been several studies done by Liberian scholars that support this argument. Mr. Ijoma Flemister, professor of history at Ohio State University and Dr. Elwood Dunn, a political scientist and a university professor, have both written extensively on the topic.

So, what are the facts behind the formation of an African colony? Who were the major decision-makers or players? And what was their purpose for initiating this idea? To answer these questions, you have to dig into the story from the beginning: the history of slave revolt in Haiti. Rebellious African slaves, who were sick and tired of repressive treatment, gave rise to fears made by southern slaveholders in the United States and the colonizationists. I want to investigate whether there would ever have been a nation called Liberia without the events of 1791. It was during that period when enslaved Africans in Haiti overthrew their owners. This was clearly a rude awakening for policymakers and southern white slaveholders in the United States. An African colony comprising of six settlements were formed, in no small part, by the influence of the colonizationists, doubtless and fearful of a similar revolt in the United States. Of the six organizations that eventually became the Republic of Liberia, the American Colonization Society (ACS) became the mother organization for the overall goal of creating an African colony of the United States. ACS members successfully collaborated with the United States government in supporting the effort, both politically and financially. The ACS was a philanthropic organization that established the settlements. In the ensuing years, the ACS and the US government continued to collaborate in sending free American blacks to Liberia. Because of the tremendous work done by ACS members, most of whom were leaders in the settlements, consequently, many of Liberia's streets and cities were named in their honor.

Obviously, some of the events in US–Liberian history were not always positive. The last part of the book explores the time period from World War I to the present, which saw many ups and downs between the United States and Liberia.

Since I see things through the lens of an educator and a political scientist, it is also from the latter perspective that this book is written, seeking to answer specific, sociological questions: How do people think and behave, both politically and culturally? How do decisions shape the outcome of people's destiny? What does it cost to sacrifice one's own future for a better future for others? The history of Liberia, with respect to the involvement of the United States, has much to do with these kinds of questions. The colonizationists must have thought about these concerns before taking their actions. And so, we will grapple with them here.

To give a full picture of Liberia, I tried to take a panoramic view of social dynamics amongst the people, researching their appetite as a nation to find their own voice, both abroad and at home. The United States played a major part in this history from the very foundation of Liberia, whether it was defending Liberia against the British and French over boundary issues, giving millions of dollars in loans and aid during hard economic times, or by resettling more than a hundred and fifty thousand Liberian refugees (during and after the civil war) in the United States, an initiative that began in 1989 and continues to the current time.

While it is true that there is criticism about the US's role in Liberia in one of the chapters in this book, the fact is that the United States has always been and continues to be a major player in the political, cultural, and social transformation of Liberia. The middle and closing chapters provide a chronological framework of US/Liberian relations, the political and social dynamics of Liberia, an outlook of Liberian culture, lifestyles, and diversity of the people, in addition to other relevant information about the country and people, including a timeline of major events in Liberian history.

Finally, I hope that readers walk away from reading this book with a question for more inquiry or an answer: Who is the actual beneficiary of the more than-two-hundred-year-old history between the United States of America and the Republic of Liberia? Whatever your answer is, the question should at least start a conversation that is worth giving close attention.

Chapter One

How It All Started

Putting history in a proper setting, it can be argued that the return of freed American blacks to Africa was neither a voluntary act nor an accident by the founders. The idea to repatriate freed American blacks to Africa had economic, political, and security implications on both continents. Research shows that the United States was the number one slave-trading nation in the world until the Jefferson Anti-Slavery Act of 1803 and the Way Showing Act of 1807. While it is true that slave trade in the United States before the industrial revolution primarily served an economic purpose, especially in the South, returning blacks to Africa was compelled, from the perspective of the men who sponsored the creation of an African colony.

The idea of sending free African Americans to Africa took a center stage after several key foreign and domestic events of the late eighteenth century, relating to slavery, hastened the process. The primary foreign event that influenced the idea of repatriation was the Haitian revolution of 1791, which was led by black leader Francois Dominique Toussaint L'Ouverture. He led fellow slaves in a revolt against their slave-masters in Santo Domingo and won their freedom. The slave rebellion lunched on August 22, 1791, represented the culmination of a conspiracy among black slave leaders on the French colony (van der Kraaij/Bremen, 1983, p. 23).

According to historical accounts of the rebellion that have been told through the years, Francois Dominique Toussaint L'Ouverture helped plot the uprising. Among the rebellion leaders were Boukman, a *Maroon* (runaway slave subsisting in community with other runaways) voodoo *hougan* (high priest), Georges Biassou, who later made Toussaint his aide in their struggle for freedom; Jean-Francois, who subsequently commanded forces along with Biassou and Toussaint under the Spanish flag, and Jeannot, the most bloodthirsty of them all. The carnage that wreaked havoc in the northern settlements of Acul, Limbe, Flaville, and Le Normand revealed the simmering fury of an oppressed people. The runaway slaves slaughtered every white person they encountered (Blackburn, Robin. *The Overthrow of Colonial Slavery,* 2004).

According to the US Department of State-Foreign Policy Agenda, (Bureau of Public Affairs) 2010, the rebellion left an estimated ten thousand black slaves and twenty-four thousand whites dead and more than one thousand plantations sacked and razed. During the ten-day rebellion, the slaves managed to take full control of the entire northern province in an unprecedented slave revolt that left the whites in control of only a few fortified camps. According to one account of the incident, the slaves sought revenge on their masters through "pillage, rage, torture, mutilation, and death."

Because the white plantation owners had long feared a revolt like this, they were well-armed and prepared to defend themselves should an attack happen. They retaliated by massacring black prisoners as they were being escorted back to town by French soldiers. Within week, approximately one hundred slaves joined the revolt, and as the violence escalated over the next two months, insurgent slaves killed two thousand whites and burned or destroyed 180 sugar plantations and hundreds of coffee and indigo plantations.

By 1792, the African slaves had control of a third of the island, a situation that created major problems for the newly elected legislative assembly of France. In order to protect France's economic interests, the legislative assembly granted civil and political rights to "free men of color" in the colonies. Many Haitians believed that the Maroons' attacks were only the first manifestation of a revolt against the French and, potentially, the entire slaveholding system. Certainly, the 1791 rebellion was a turning point that evolved into the Haitian revolution. The event marked the beginning of a martial tradition (martial tradition means that the event was suited for war or military life) for blacks, just as service in the colonial militia had done for the *gens de couleur* ("free people of color," one of the four types of people in Haiti).

News of the incident spread like a wide fire around the world, including the United States. The fear and uncertainty among whites in America was that Toussaint, a full-blooded African who had defeated British and French forces, might eventually invade the United States and free the slaves; alternatively, free African Americans might follow or join Toussaint in freeing their brothers and sisters from captivity in this country. This sentiment was more prevalent in the southern part of the United States, where the general thought had been that the Haitian revolution could spell similar disasters here on the mainland. Haiti had an official policy to accept any black person who arrived on their shores as a citizen.

The legislatures of Pennsylvania and South Carolina, as well as Washington, DC, sent help to the French whites of Saint-Dominique, Haiti. According to Blackburn in his article "Haiti's Slavery in the Age of the Democratic Revolution" (William and Mary Quarterly; 63.4, 633–644, 2006), studies on the history of the Haitian Revolution, there was debate over whether the United States should institute an embargo against Haiti. John Taylor of South Carolina spoke for much of the popular sentiment among the leaders from the South during that time. To Taylor, the Haitian revolution exemplified that slavery should be permanently institutionalized in the United States. He further argued against the idea that slavery had caused the revolution in Haiti by suggesting that the antislavery movement had provoked the revolt in the first place.

According to historian Tim Mathewson, John Taylor's comments in the debate shows how people's attitude had changed in the South from one of reluctantly accepting slavery as a necessity to one of seeing it as a fundamental aspect of Southern culture and the planter class. As the years progressed, Haiti had only become a bigger target for scorn amongst the pro-slavery factions in the South. The belief among many southern whites was that the revolution through violence in Haiti was an inherent characteristic of blacks, as proved by the slaughtering of French whites and the authoritarian rule that followed at the end of the revolution.

"The Battle on Santo Domingo," (a painting by January Suchodolski, depicting a struggle between Polish troops in French service and the Haitian rebels) 2006

"A Massacre of 1791" Revenge by the black troops for cruelty of French soldiers: (Courtesy of Wikipedia, the Free Encyclopedia)

The fearful white slaveholders called the will of the slaves to free themselves the "Santo Domingo virus," a sickness whites believed arrived on slave ships from the West Indies. It was thought that the revolutionary forces set off by the Haitian revolution—on the island that encompassed Santo Domingo, the present-day Dominican Republic, and Saint-Domingue, present-day Haiti—were infecting the American slave population and inciting insurrection. The white Americans were concerned that a race war was imminent. In the 1800s, there was an alarming increase in the number of free African Americans in the United States. Although the ratio of whites to blacks was 8:2 from 1790 to 1800, it was the massive increase in the number of *free* African Americans that disturbed the colonizationists. From 1790 to 1800, the number of free African Americans increased from 59,467 to 108,378, a percentage increase of 82 percent; and from 1800 to 1810, the number increased from 108,378 to 186,446, an increase of 72 percent. While colonizationists in the south were motivated by racism and fear of a slave uprising, colonizationists in the north refused to accept the notion of white–black coexistence. The final solution would be to have this class of people deported from United States.

Situation before the Slave Revolt

According to an account from Haiti before the uprising in 1791, the African-born slaves lived in terrible conditions, oppressed and treated as if they were less human. In 1789, the colony of Saint-Domingue was producing 40 percent of the world's sugar. Not only was it France's most profitable and wealthiest colony, it was the period's most flourishing slave colony in the Caribbean. There were three classes of people: whites, free people of color (gens de couleur or mulattoes), and the enslaved blacks, who outnumbered the whites and the people of color by eight to one. The slave population on the island totaled five hundred thousand by 1789, according to Bob Corbett, a Haitian historian, almost half of the one million slaves in the Caribbean. The slaves were mostly first generation African-born. The death rate in the Caribbean exceeded the birth rate; as a result, kidnapped Africans continued to be imported as slaves to meet the demand for labor on the plantations. At the same time, the adult slave population declined at an annual rate of 2–5 percent, due to deaths caused by exhaustion. The slaves also had inadequate food and shelter, no clothing or medical care, as well as an imbalance of the sexes, the men outnumbering the women, Corbett, (2009). Some of the slaves were of a Creole language (Creole is a language spoken by more than twelve million along with French in Haiti), elite class born in the urban areas and served in domestic capacities as cooks, personal servants, and artisans around the plantation house. They were a relatively privileged class who were chiefly born in the Americas (the Creole-speaking Haitians were equivalent to "house Negros" in the United States during the period of slavery; Haitian slaves and their descendents who did not work on the plantations).

The underclass of African-born slaves were confined to hard labor and abusive conditions. On the island of Saint-Domingue in 1789, the population of whites was about forty thousand. The sugar planters, known as the *grands blancs,* or "rich whites," were chiefly minor aristocratic Frenchmen. This group usually returned to France as soon as possible when their assignments were over to avoid the dreaded, tropical yellow-fever disease, which regularly swept the colony. The lower-class whites, also known as *petit blancs, or* "minor whites," included artisans, shopkeepers, slave dealers, overseers, and day laborers. The island of Saint-Dominique's free people of color known as *the gens de couleur libres*, with a total population of twenty-eight thousand by 1789, was what is known in America as a biracial population. Many of them served as artisans and overseers or domestic servants in the big houses (Corbert, 2009).

There were other issues among the three groups in addition to the class and racial tension between whites, free people of color, and the enslaved blacks. The island was polarized by regional rivalries between regions in the north, the south, and the west. There were also conflicts between proponents of independence: those loyal to France, the allies of Spain, and the allies of Great Britain, all of whom desired control over this valuable colony. With such polarization, it is obvious that uprising was inevitable; there was discontent among the African slaves who were going through abuse both physical and emotional at the time.

Laws and Regulations Enacted in the United States in Reaction to the Haitian Revolt

Between 1794 and 1800, the US federal government passed anti-slave-trade laws to prevent the possible spread of the Haitian slave revolt to its shores. The first act prohibited citizens from equipping ships engaged in slave-trade commerce; the second prohibited Americans from serving aboard such ships or from having any interest in their voyages (Aptheker, (1993): 45). Beginning in 1792, southern states like South Carolina, Kentucky, North Carolina, Georgia, and Maryland passed laws restricting slave trade as a means of preventing the possible *infection* of the country by the Haitian rebellion.

South Carolina's statute prohibited the importation by any one person of more than two slaves and required that the slaves imported be for personal use only. This law was subsequently modified to retain a total ban only with respect to slaves from the West Indies or South America. However, all imported slaves had to be accompanied by a statement signed by two magistrates attesting that the slaves had not been involved in any insurrection or revolt (Aptheker, (1993): 73–74).

In 1797, Baltimore, Maryland, passed an ordinance declaring all slaves imported from the West Indies between 1792 and 1797 to be "dangerous to the peace and welfare of the city" and ordering their masters to banish them (Aptheker, (1993): 74).

Many southern states enacted measures restricting the civil liberties of blacks, including laws forbidding meetings of slaves without the presence of whites, prohibiting the assembly of blacks on city streets after dark, requiring slaves to have passes when off plantation, forbidding slaves to possess weapons, and providing severe penalties for sedition.

Aptheker also points out the South Carolina regulation that made it necessary for a magistrate and five freeholders to approve a document of *manumission* or liberation from slavery, freeing slaves from bondage. One of the stated reasons for this regulation was a concern that slaveholders would release slaves "of bad or depraved character" who might incite rebellion once freed.

Freed blacks were restricted in their rights to hold certain jobs or learn certain trades that might make it easier for them to organize a rebellion. They were also restricted in their freedom of movement from state to state or county to county. In some states, blacks were prevented from testifying in court against white persons; this restriction had the effect of preventing blacks from defending themselves against charges that they were part of a slave conspiracy.

Shortly after the Vesey Plot to burn down Charleston, North Carolina, was aborted, white Carolinians took measure to ensure that free blacks were given even less freedom. (Dermark Vessy was a convicted plotter in the 1822 slaves rebellion; Vessy, along with thirty-four other blacks, were hanged in what historians believed to be the largest civil execution in United States' history.) As part of the effort, in December 1832, the South Carolina legislature enacted the Free-Colored Seamen's Act, requiring that all free blacks employed on incoming vessels be detained in jail while their ship was in port.

Chapter Two

Establishment of the American Colonization Society (ACS)

The common belief that Liberia was founded by freed American slaves in 1847 must be challenged. An argument can be made that Liberia was founded by people other than free African Americans, namely the American white men who organized as the American Colonization Society (ACS) and established Liberia in 1821.

The ACS was inaugurated on December 21, 1816, in Washington, D.C., by American political and religious leaders who formulated the idea of creating an African colony. They included the following dignitaries:

President James Monroe

President Thomas Jefferson

President James Madison

Speaker of the House of Representatives Henry Clay of Kentucky

Chief Justice John Marshall of the United States Supreme Court

Secretary of the Treasury William H. Crawford of Georgia

Attorney General William Hirt

Associate Supreme Court Justice Bushrod Washington (nephew of President George Washington)

President (and general) Andrew Jackson of Tennessee

Elias B. Caldwell, clerk of the United States Supreme Court

Congressman Charles Fenton Mercer of Virginia

Daniel Webster of Massachusetts

Francis Scott Key, author of the Star-Spangled Banner, the US national anthem

John Taylor of Virginia

Richard Rush, who served as United States Minister of England

Rev. Robert Finley

All of the ACS members were white gentlemen who happened to be either slaveholders or subscribed to the preservation of the institution of slavery—except Rev. Robert Finley, who did not own slaves according to historical account. For the creation of ACS, much credit is given to Rev. Robert Finley (1772-1817, who died at the age of forty-five), a white American clergyman. Born in Princeton, New Jersey in 1772; and graduated from the College of New Jersey (now Princeton University) in 1787, where he also studied theology. Finley was ordained in 1795 and served for more than twenty years at Basking Ridge, New Jersey, both as a pastor and headmaster of a school of boys. Finley's interest in the condition of American blacks led him to lobby for the establishment of an organization that would help freed slaves return to Africa. His dream was realized in 1816 with the establishment of the American Colonization Society at Washington, DC. There would not have been an ACS or the idea of creating an African colony without the man whose humanitarian cause resulted into the creation of a nation.

Admittedly, the creation of an African colony was first conceived by an improbable group of three other men: they met and planned on collaborating but Samuel Hopkins died before the vision was realized. Rev. Samuel Hopkins, a slave owner and trader from Rhode Island; Bristol Yamma, an African American church leader; and John Quamine, a former slave. However, the vision of these men failed because of lack of funding. Then, a wealthy black ship owner, Paul Cuffe, came along and, under a British initiative, transported the first group of eighty-eight free African Americans in 1815 to Sherbro Island, near Freetown, Sierra Leone. Paul Cuffe was a wealthy African American and ship owner who planned to transport free blacks to Africa. Paul Cuffe had similar plan for African Americans but not a part of ACS.

For their part, members of ACS had a four-step plan, which included the following: (1) all free African Americans were to either emigrate freely or be deported to Liberia; (2) the slave trade was to be abolished to stop the influx of more Africans into the United States; (3) the institution of slavery was to be preserved; and (4) as African Americans were released from slavery, they were to be deported directly to Liberia.

According to Barton Seth, author of the article "Remarks on the Colonization of the Western Coast of Africa," Cornell University Library, the views of the ACS to repatriate free African Americans back to Africa were unambiguously conspicuous in their writings, inextricably binding class and race together into a dead end.

President James Monroe, who was governor of Virginia when the abortive attempt had been made by the slaves in Charleston, North Carolina, in 1822, wrote, "Unhappily, while this class of people [former slaves] exists among us, we can never count with certainty on its tranquil submission."

Chief Justice John Marshall wrote, "The removal of our color population is I think, a common object, by no means confined to the slave states."

President James Madison wrote that "the blacks ought to be permanently removed beyond the region occupied by or allotted to a white population."

Henry Clay said, "Of all classes of our population, the most vicious is that of the free colored … if the principle of colonization should be confined to them; if a colony can be firmly established and successfully continued in Africa … much good will be done" (Barton, (1850) p. 12).

Francis Scott Key wrote, "Any scheme of emancipation without colonization, [the slaves holders] know and see and feel to be productive of nothing but evil."

President Thomas Jefferson said, "Their amalgamation with other color produces a degradation to which no lover of this country, no lover of excellence in human character, can innocently consent."

Ralph Randolph Gurley, one of the leaders of the ACS and one of the founders of the Liberian settlement *and* the man after whom Gurley Street in Monrovia is named, said the following about the abolition of slavery and the ultimate separation of the races in his book *Life of Jehudi Ashmun:* "The friends of African Colonizationists have thought, that the consents of the South were indispensable for the safety of abolition of slavery; that the work should be done with caution and preparation; that circumstances and consequences should be regarded; that a separation of races so distinct as the colored and white in complexion, habits and conditions are desirable for the happiness of both."

From the writing of the members of ACS, it is clear that there was definite purpose for the creation of the American Colonization Society

(ACS): not as is commonly believed, for the restitutional establishment of an African colony for free blacks, but for security reasons in the interest of Southern slaveholders, as well as the advancement of racial separation.

In 1816, Henry Clay, then Speaker of the House of Representatives, and other leading colonizationists met in Washington, DC, and agreed to form the American Colonization Society. Subsequently, the ACS elected Associate Justice Bushrod Washington as its president. Thirteen vice presidents were also elected, including Henry Clay, future president General Andrew Jackson, and Secretary of the Treasury William Crawford. Francis Scott Key was one of the twelve men elected to manage the day-to-day affairs of the organization; Elias Caldwell was elected its secretary. The original goal of the colonizationist movement, according to the ACS constitution, was to assist free African Americans who wanted to voluntarily immigrate to their ancestral home in Africa; paraphrasing in this assertion.

When the news of the idea reached African American leaders that slaveholders were planning a colony for them in Africa, they met for a meeting in Philadelphia and issued a statement to oppose the idea. It is not known the number of black leaders that met in Philedelphia to oppose the idea of an African colony. Despite the leaders' opposition, the ACS went ahead with its plan. To assure the success of the scheme, the ACS and some Southern slaveholders formulated an agreement to turn over all manumitted (legally freed) African Americans to the ACS, so that they would be deported to the colony in Africa. Any manumitted slave who refused to emigrate was to be resold into slavery (Berlin, Ira (1974): p. 20).

In 1818, the ACS commissioned two white Americans, Samuel J. Mills and Ebenezer Burgess, to proceed to England and Sierra Leone and gather information on the settlement of an African American colony on the west coast of Africa. In England, the two men met with Lord Bathurst, Secretary of State for Colonial Affairs, and His Royal Highness William Federick, president of the African Institution. After gaining support of the British government, which was stipulated in a letter to the British governor in Sierra Leone and leaders of the American Colonization Society (ACS), Mills and Burgess went to Sierra Leone.

Shortly after their arrival in Sierra Leone, Ebenezer Burgess was infected with malaria (or yellow fever) and died. Mills continued the journey and returned to the United States with positive results, reporting to the ACS that establishment of an African American colony on the west coast of Africa was possible. In February 1820, the vessel *Elizabeth* was charted by the US government and departed with eighty-three African Americans for Sierra Leone.

According to US Library of Congress research, these African Americans were not forced to make the expedition or emigrate to Africa. Shortly after their arrival, all of the white agents and nineteen African Americans perished from exposure to various tropical diseases. The letters they wrote back to the United States to friends and relatives about conditions on the ground further escalated fear among African Americans, preventing more from making the decision to return to Africa.

Why would someone want to go to a place where conditions are uncertain for them? After decades in the United States, if not their entire lives, they had learned to cope with the weather and social conditions. Many African Americans had serious reservations about going back to Africa. Some argued that they had helped to build America—why would they leave to go to a place with no known culture or language, and uncertain social connections? Some of these arguments remain true up to this day; the descendants of those who went to Liberia speak only English and have little or no cultural connections to Africa. Others managed to assimilate with indigenous Africans through marriage and other forms of association, making it much easier for them to learn the African way of life.

The Settlement of Monrovia

To ensure the success of the ACS, the US Congress passed an Act on March 3, 1819, authorizing President James Monroe the sum of $100,000 to provide "logistics for the establishment of an African colony" (Levy (2005) p.81). Liberia's capital, Monrovia, is named after President Monroe for his role in the formation of the country. Negotiations between representatives of ACS, the government of the United States, and indigenous African leaders resulted in the purchase of "Dozoa Island and all portions of the land bounded north and west by the Atlantic Ocean, and on the south and east by a line drawn in a south-east direction from the north of [the] Mesurado River" … thus, Liberia was established.

13

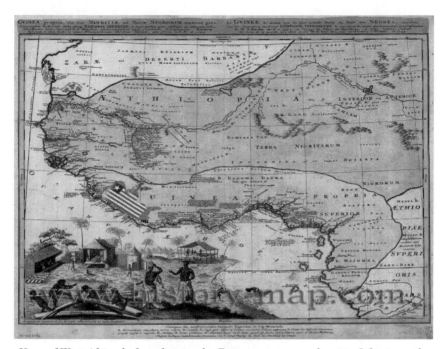

*View of West Africa before division by European powers showing Liberia as the
only independent nation (courtesy of Wikipedia, the Free Encyclopedia).*

In 1821, the US government again chartered another vessel, the
USS *Nautilus,* to carry a group of African Americans to Sierra Leone.
The mission was led by J. B. Winn; Ephraim Bacon represented the US
government; and Joseph R. Andrus represented the ACS. Andrus and
Bacon visited various coastal areas, including present-day Liberia, but
were unsuccessful in working out a treaty with the indigenous people
there. Due to a series of failures and mounting costs, the ACS turned to
the US government for help.

"In a favorable response, President James Monroe ordered Captain
Robert F. Stockton of the United Sates Navy to visit the west coast of
Africa" (Franklin, (1969), p. 686).

In December, Captain Stockton arrived in Sierra Leone in his
newly commissioned vessel, the USS *Alligator,* and proceeded to Cape
Montserrado with Dr. Eli Ayres, the ACS agent, to negotiate for land. In a
series of incidents on present-day Bushrod Island, a suburb of Monrovia,
Captain Stockton forced indigenous leaders of the cape, including one

King Peter (whose African name is unknown), at the barrel of a gun to sign a treaty ceding their lands to the African American settlers.

The first few years after their arrival (both in Sierra Leone and Liberia) were very challenging for the settlers. They suffered from malaria and yellow fever, diseases that are common in coastal plains and mangrove swamps. All three agents and twenty-two of the original colonists died from malaria, yellow fever, and other tropical diseases. Between 1820 and 1843, diseases killed about 22 percent of all new arrivals.

In addition, tensions were building between the surviving colonists and their leaders, as well as between the resettled African Americans and local African natives. Those early governors, all of whom were white men picked by the ACS, maintained an autocratic style of leadership over the freed slaves that had left the United States to escape oppression. The black settlers had no interest in continued domination by the American Colonization Society on what was purported to be their own home continent. Settlers were also periodically attacked by native populations who were unhappy with the expansion of settlements along the coastal areas. The settlers were also determined to put an end to the lucrative slave trade, with which the native populations were intimately involved.

The new nation was faced with instability caused by the fight between the settlers and the native populations. The settlers were determined to create and develop a nation run for and by them. Having assimilated to Western culture, they now attempted to Christianize the communities of native populations, despite the difficulties in doing so. Ironically, the settlers, many of whom had once been in bondage, began to discriminate against the native Africans, whom they considered uncivilized, at least, during that time. Natives were excluded from voting and kept out of government. This basic ignorance was so conspicuous that in the country's Declaration of Independence, they asserted their superiority blatantly, in the following words: "We the people of Liberia were originally inhabitants of the United States of North America."

These practices led to fighting between the settlers (known as Americo-Liberians) and the sixteen ethnic African tribes that lived in the area before their arrival. The turmoil between the settlers and the native populations discouraged prospective immigrants from the United States to Liberia. Edward Blyden, an Americo-Liberian who became a successful writer and speaker, mourned the promise for which his country once stood. He wrote, "We are keeping these lands, we say, for our brethren in America ... but they are not willing to come." There was no specific timeline to illustrate that Edward Blyden's comment was made in the early 1800s or in the 1890s.

By 1824, the settlement had survived and was named Monrovia after the fifth US president, James Monroe (1816–1824), one of the ACS members. Over the next forty years, nineteen thousand African Americans repatriated to Liberia, along with five thousand Africans who were rescusd from a slave ship, and a small number of West Indies immigrants. Today, the settlement of Monrovia serves as the political and commercial capital of Liberia.

Most of the rescued Africans who were brought from the Congo (now Congo-Brazzaville) and central Africa settled in Bushrod Island, Monrovia, an island that was named after American politician Bushrod Washington, another member of the ACS and a nephew of George Washington. Some of the Congo people were settled in a place that is present day Congo Town, a suburb of Monrovia.

Over time, relations between the settlers and the native populations would improve. In Liberia today, one can hardly tell the difference between native populations and settlers. People live anywhere they wish in Liberia. Education and intermarriages contributed to the removal of barriers and divisions. The policy of Unification and Integration by President William V. S. Tubman, who served from 1944 until his death in 1971, also contributed to the breakdown of barriers between different groups in Liberia; especially the indigenous populations and the Americo-Liberians.

The Congo people were the largest group of captured African slaves who were brought to Liberia. As these Africans were brought to Liberia, they were handed over to the Americo-Liberians, who then changed their African names to Western names. Copying their American experience, when African slaves were compelled to take on the names of their slaves masters, the Americo-Liberians changed the names of the African slaves to that of their last names; so that eventually every rescused African slaves to Libberia also had Western names like the Americo-Liberians.

Gradually, these rescued African slaves became absorbed by the lower strata of the Americo-Liberians and eventually formed one group. The process was not only through the social and political rise of the Congos within the Americo-Liberians group, but also through a breakdown of the barriers to intermarriage within the social orders. Another trend developed as skin color became increasingly less important in defining social status and prestige among Liberians in the twentieth century.

The Americo-Liberians placed an emphasis on the differences between themselves and the indigenous people. Today in Liberia, the phrases "Congo people" and "Americo-Liberians" are used interchangeably to refer to the descendents of free American slaves from America and the rescued African slaves taken from smugglers after slave trading was abolished in 1808. Most often, the identification can be established by family name; usually last names.

The word Congo has three categories. The first category refers to the descendents of African slaves who were brought from the Congo and diverted to Liberia by British and American navy ships. The second category refers to Americo-Liberians or descendents of free, American blacks who later joined with the Africans from the Congo—the Congo, according to historical account, coming from an area where the largest number of African slaves were traded to the Americas. The third category refers to the native children, those with an indigenous background, who were educated by the Americo-Liberians. That third category of Congo, according to Liberian culture, are those considered *civilized* (or Congo) due to their social status in society. Consequently, over a period of years, descendents of all groups were the same culturally and socially.

The Americo-Liberians taught these newly arriving Africans to speak English and to live like the Americo-Liberians. The Americo-Liberians also taught the Africans from the Congo and elsewhere their style of architectural design, which was very similar to how houses were built in the southern parts of the United States. All along the coastal cities and towns, Southern plantation housing style or designs still exist today in Liberia.

According to Mr. Joseph Johnson, former associate professor at the University of Liberia, now residing in Minnesota, the Africans from the Congo were settled in Bushrod Island and Congo Town, all suburbs of Monrovia, and eventually handed over to the Americo-Liberians as house servants or taken to work on their farms.

Some of the Africans from the Congo were sent to farms like Clay-Ashland, named after Henry Clay, (one of the founders of ACS and Jehudi Ashmun, former governor of the settlement of Monrovia. Other Africans from the Congo worked as servants at plantations like Lott Carey, Caldwell, and other nearby areas around the City of Monrovia.

Most of these areas have now developed into cities of their own. It is fair to argue that the word Congo is very relative today in Liberia, because it encompasses anyone who is a "civilized person" or lives like a civilized person.

In a personal correspondence with Professor Johnson, he explained that the word Congo becoming dominant as the positive word for accruing status was a number one game during that period. Because the Congo population represented the largest group of settlers—and since democracy is about numbers—he pointed out that it served the interests of the Americo-Liberians to accrue status to that part of Africa; to them, creating a new, homogenous society. Aspiring to "be Congo," Africans who came from Ghana, Nigeria, Sierra Leone, and other parts of Africa also accentuated the values and principles of the population that became the most educated and prominent and influential group in the Liberian society.

During the ensuing years, the ACS and the American government continued to send African Americans to Liberia. Between 1818 and 1838, several settlements were established along the Grain Coast of West Africa under the sponsorship of societies such as:

American Colonization Society
Maryland State Colonization Society
New York Colonization Society
Virginia Colonization Society
Kentucky Colonization Society
Mississippi State Colonization Society

The ACS took over the leadership of all these efforts, which brought all the other organizations into one entity. In the Liberian history, the ACS is the only group known when it comes to the creation of an African colony. The US government also delegated to the ACS with responsibilities and decision-making authority, ranging from the appointment of governors for the colony to the drafting of the constitution. The ACS had the most prominent members who were also part of the US government.

Commonwealth of Liberia

In 1824, the ACS drafted a constitution for the colony, and on January 5, 1839, the settlements were united into one government under the name Commonwealth of Liberia. Realistically, it was the Commonwealth of the United States but was known as the Commonwealth of Liberia). The commonwealth was led by a white governor named Thomas Buchanan, after whom the second largest city in Liberia was named. Thomas Buchanan was the first governor of the Commonwealth of Liberia.

Buchanan served from January 1839 through September 1841. Prior to this appointment, he served as agent of the Pennsylvania and New York Colonization Societies in Bassa Cove. Bassa Cove was later renamed Buchanan in his honor. He died in September 1841, after he was infected with "the fever"—either malaria or yellow fever. Governor Buchanan was buried in Monrovia.

Buchanan was succeeded by Joseph Jenkins Roberts, the first African American governor of the commonwealth. Of the subsequent eleven governors of the commonwealth, six were American white men and five were freeborn American black men. In 1847, after a series of commercial conflicts with British traders, including Britain's refusal to recognize Liberia's sovereignty under the existing modus operandi, Governor Roberts and his comrades—all successful merchants financially impaired by the British action—asked and received permission from the ACS to declare Liberia an independent nation. (The US government operated through the ACS since most of the founding members of ACS were US government officials.) On July 26, 1847, Liberia became an independent nation.

Reasons for the Declaration of Independence

Twenty-six years after the colony was established might seem too soon to talk about sovereignty, but in 1842, the British vessel HMS *Lily* invaded the Port of Buchanan, Liberia's second-largest city, which had become the commonwealth's primary harbor. The British seized the ship *John Seys,* owned by future Liberian president Steven Allen Benson, an African American, under the charge of "suspicion of slave-trading." (The ship *John Seys* was the personal property of President Steven Allen Benson; therefore, identification of country letters was not necessary.)

The British action was in retaliation of a seizure of British ship, the HMS *Little Ben,* by Liberia for violating Liberian custom regulations. Britain demanded reparations from Benson for the return of the *John Seys,* but Benson refused to accede to the demand. As a result, the vessel and cargo were auctioned off by the British government.

When the ACS protested the British action, they replied with, "Great Britain could not recognize the sovereign powers of Liberia, which she regarded as a mere commercial experiment of a philanthropic society."

Because of the halfhearted reply of the British government, the US Department of State launched a movement to "declare the Commonwealth of Liberia a Free, Sovereign and Independent State, under the name and style of The Republic of Liberia" (Library of Congress (2001) p. 16). Commonwealth Governor Joseph Jenkins Roberts, Steven Allen Benson, and the rest of their merchant comrades also received permission from the ACS to accomplish their goal of an "Independent Republic."

There were several other incidents in addition to the seizure of the *John Seys,* Steven Allen Benson's ship, that caused Liberia to declare its independence. They include: (a) the Nat Turner insurrection in Southampton County, Virginia, in 1831, which forced the ACS to accelerate its grand design by emigrating 633 freeborn black men to Liberia. It took a total of seven ships, costing $73,886 (an equivalent of $2.3 million in 2010 dollars) to transport these men, an expense that put the ACS into bankruptcy. (b) Henry Clay, who had made political enemies by denying the American presidency to future US president Andrew Jackson in 1842 and successfully opposing the appointment of Martin Van Buren as United Sates Minister to Britain, was elected president of ACS in 1835. Andrew Jackson (1829–1837) and Martin Van Buren (1837–1841) both became president of the United Sates and retaliated against Clay by substantially reducing the United States' role in Liberia. And (c) the US financial crisis that became known as the Panic of 1836 and began a five-year Depression substantially reduced donations to the ACS, further contributing to its bankruptcy. All these events, particularly the bankruptcy, forced the Liberian leaders to declare the Commonwealth of Liberia an Independent, Free, and Sovereign State on July 26, 1847. Paradoxically, Great Britain, France, Prussia, and Belgium accorded recognition to the Republic of Liberia before the United States did. It would take another fifteen years before Liberia was officially recognized under President Abraham Lincoln's administration.

Chapter Three

Before the Arrival of African Americans in Liberia

Prior to the arrival of the first group of African Americans to this part of Africa in 1821, there were great kingdoms: Songhai, Mali (not present-day Mali), and Ghana (not present-day Ghana) along the great coastal lands in the areas of West Africa known as Upper Guinea Coast and the Grain Coast, which is present-day Liberia. These kingdoms fell, leaving a dozen or so ethnic groups in their wake.

Anthropologists have divided the various ethnic groups inhabiting this land into three linguistic groups:

Mande (Mande-Tan and Mande-Fu) this is one linguistic group according to Liberian history

Mel

Kru

The Mande Tan consisted of the Vai and Mandingo peoples, originally inhabiting the Quoja Kingdom. (The Quoja Kingdom used to exist in the area before the arrival of the Mande-Tan group.) This kingdom extended from the present-day Mano River to Cape Mesurado. The related Mane-Fu language comprises the Mano (Maa), Gio (Dan), Gbee, Loma, Gbande, and the Kpelle peoples. These speakers occupied the Nimba (Noonva) and the Lofa regions.

The second group, Mel, comprises the Gola and the Kissi. The Gola inhabited the interior part of the Quoja kingdom, which was ruled by King Manu.

The Kru linguistic group is composed of the Bassa, Grebo, Dey, Krahn, Sapo, and Kru or Krao-speaking people. They occupied the Folgier kingdom, extending from the area now called Monrovia, the capital of Liberia, to the Saint Paul River. The Kru is a semi-Bantu linguistic group of the Kwia-speaking family. As an ethnic tribal group, they are called the Krao people. These name are spelled differently by different ethnic groups; an example is the Dan tribe in the Nimba County (in north eastern Liberia) commonly known as the Gio tribe.

From the vicinity of Monrovia where they originally resided, the Krao people gradually migrated southeast into the coastal areas. The Bassa, on the other hand, lived east of the St. Paul River. The Krahn occupied the southeastern interior of Liberia and the mid-western parts of present-day Ivory Coast. They are called Guere in the Ivory Coast. The Ivorian Krahn (Guere) and the Liberian Krahn are the same people, only separated by the Cavala River. The same relationship exists between the Liberian Gio (Dan) and the Ivorian Gio (Yakoba).

The Kru-speaking peoples arrived on the Grain Coast about AD 850. The Kru, a subdivision of the Krahn-Dan Kingdom, broke away from Dan Kingdom after Islamic mercenaries from Goa and Jenne invaded the kingdom in about AD 700. (The Krahn-Dan is the name of a kingdom within the Kru-speaking people.) Prior to their arrival, Hanno of Carthage had visited the area in 520 BC. Historical records indicate that he did not find traders on the Grain Coast.

The Greboes are a subdivision of the Krahn-speaking peoples that includes the interior Greboes of Liberia as well as the coastal and interior Greboes of Ivory Coast. The Greboes arrived in Liberia in about AD 965. They are also related to a subgroup of Dei, Bassa, Belle, Krahns, and Kru-proper in Liberia. This group is linguistically related to the Betes, Wuobe, Krahn, Didas, Neon, Klepos, Baapos, Ulebos, Plaapos, Tepo, and the Bakwe in the Ivory Coast. (These names are sometimes spelled differently between Liberia and the Ivory Coast.)

The Bassa, Dey, Gola, and Vai, representing all three linguistic families, encountered the first group of African Americans. After the departure of Captain Stockton, Dey, Gola, and Vai warriors formed an alliance and attempted to forcibly evict the settlers. Upon hearing about the imminent threat to the existence of the African Americans, Dr. Eli Ayres (who was a physician and the first agent of the American colonization Society in what would later become Liberia), appealed for help from King Sabsu—also known as King Sao and Boatswain (his real name was Sao, and Bsu was the way his people pronounced Boatswain) (*Journal of Black Studies*, Vol. 23 no. 1 (1992) pp. 107–116)

King Sabsu was one of the most dominant indigenous leaders in the region. Sabsu was a Mandingo king and a devoted Muslim. He married a Gola woman, who bore him four sons; among whom was Momoru Sao, who ruled Bopulu in the 1860s.

Sabsu was from Bopulu, a northwestern region of the country in present-day Lofa County. Called Bokoma by Sabsu's people, Bopulu was a hundred miles from the coast. (Bokoma was a leader and chief of the Sabsu people from Bopulu.) Like other African warriors, Sabsu people raided towns and villages from Cape Mount to Bassa, a distance of about two hundred miles along the coast, and sold his victims into slavery. Nonetheless, King Sabsu is most remembered in the Liberian history for his honesty.

In the 1822 crisis between African Americans and Dey, Gola and Vai kings, Sabsu arrived on the coast with a massive force and warned the indigenous rulers that he would behead anyone who interfered with the Americans. He told the African American settlers, "I promise you my full protection. If these people give you further disturbance, send for me, and I swear, if they oblige me to come again to quiet them, I will do it by taking [their] heads from their shoulders, as I did [to] old King George's on my last visit to the coast to settle disputes."

Shorty after the departure of King Sabsu for Bopulu, the Dey, Gola, and the Vai warriors attacked the African Americans' settlement. The first major battle occurred in the morning, on Monday, November 11, 1822, while the colony was under the leadership of Jehudi Ashmun, a white American from Champlain, New York. In a series of battles, no clear winner emerged, until the British governor in neighboring Sierra Leone intervened and brought to completion an uneasy peace treaty between the two groups.

The indigenous tribes that encountered the African Americans were a warring people. They had two major trades, salt and slavery, and very strong, ancient armies, which they would use to sweep up anybody they met on their way. That's how they had occupied the entire seacoast. With such a background, it was no surprise that there would be resistance in meeting the request of the African Americans for land. Additionally, the settlers wanted the indigenous people to accept their culture. This was a primary reason for the conflict between the two groups. It is believed that many of the indigenous peoples of what is known now as Liberia migrated from the north and east between the twelfth and sixteenth centuries AD. This area of West Africa was invaded in the sixteenth century by Mane Malian soldiers from tribes in what is now the interior of present-day Ivory Coast and Ghana. The Mane Malian partitioned the conquered territories and their peoples among the Mane leaders with one chieftain over all. The supreme chief resided in the Grand Cape Mount area. This is a regional story about a group of people from one generation to the other.

The Vai were part of the Mali Empire until forced to migrate when the empire collapsed in the fourteenth century. The Vai, Dey, and Gola eventually migrated to the coastal region known today as Grand Cape Mount County in Southwestern Liberia. The Kru, one of the sixteen aboriginal peoples of Liberia that lived in the interior and coastal parts of the country, had opposed the migration of the Vai. The Manes and Kru peoples created an alliance to stop further migration of the Vai, but the Vai people remained in the Grand Cape Mount region, where the capital city of Robertsport is currently located. Robertsport is the provincial capital of Grand Cape Mount County, similar to state capitals in the United States or the Federal Republic of Nigeria.

The Kru also traded with the Europeans, initially with goods only, but later became active participants in human trafficking as well. Kru traders and their canoes would be taken onboard European ships and to engage in trade along the coastal areas of what is now Liberia. At some agreeable point, the Kru traders and canoes would be put off the ships, and the traders would paddle back to their home territory. Kru laborers left their territory to work on plantations and in construction as paid laborers. Kru laborers were involved in the building of the Suez Canal in Egypt and the Panama Canal in Central America.

The Grebo people were also driven into the area as a result of the Manes or Mane Malian invasion. Portuguese explorers first made contact with West Africa, particularly what is known today as Liberia, as early as 1461. Because of the abundance of melegueta pepper, also known as Grains of Paradise for its pungent seeds, the explorers named the area the Grain Coast. Liberia is referred to as the Grain Coast to this day (from Wikipedia, the free encyclopedia; 2009).

In 1602, the Dutch established a trading post at Grand Cape Mount, but the post was later destroyed. In 1663, the British installed trading posts on the Grain Coast. There were no foreign settlements in the area until the arrival of the African Americans in 1821. However, there were some indigenous villages in the area long before the arrival of the settlers or the Americo-Liberians. When they arrived, they entered into a rich cultural mix, with at least thirteen distinctly different, coexisting to some degree and often competing tribes. This complexity still exists today. Due to intermarriage and years of communal tradition between the indigenous and immigrant groups, one can hardly tell today who is the real "Congo" and who the "Native," in spite of such complexity. The Liberian nation—much like the United States of America—is considered one of Africa's melting pots, with people from different parts of the world living as one people.

Early Social Structure of Indigenous Groups:

No strong centralized political structures remained after the fall of the three original great kingdoms, Ghana, Mali, and Songhai. Instead, power centered on royal families in which the monarch's younger brother would succeed as chief over his eldest son. In this *agnatic* seniority tradition, the next generation would not be eligible to rule until all the available elder men, brothers to the king or chief, had been exhausted. Under this, a patrilineal system, West African women were never in line to rule. Consequently, male children were preferred over female children, in view of keeping the family's name and status intact in the kingdom or tribe.

The compound or household group was the only political power that the chief and household enjoyed. While the power might have been more domestic than political, the chief still commanded an enormous amount of authority and respect. The chief also had the authority to administer and dispense law and justice. However, he could not exercise his influence in an autocratic manner, because his decisions and authority were subject to the consent and advice of powerful tribal elders. Variously named—*Poro, Sande, Zoes,* and *Bodeos*—these elders were the equivalent of high priests or priestesses and presided over rites of passage ceremonies for the younger members of the clan, as well as other crucial village matters and protocols. The high priests served as advisors in reaching important decisions that concerned the clan and its people.

With the influence of Western education, the role of women has dramatically changed over time in most parts of Africa, including Liberia, as evidenced by the current leadership of President Ellen Johnson Sirleaf of Liberia.

Secret Indigenous Societies

The purpose of this book is to tell the story in a balance way about the indigenous people and their lifestyles as well as the settlers.

Their differences aside, the pre-Liberian societies were predominantly agrarian in nature, utilizing both farming and hunting for providing food. They had strong animistic beliefs and secret, sacred societies that helped the clans maintain their equilibrium through metaphysical, if not supernatural, means. Nearly half the population of Liberia are members of one secret society or the other—Poros being the secret society for men and Sande for women. Membership included past presidents like William Tubman and his successor, William Richard Tolbert. Even through Presidents William R. Tolbert and William V.S. Tubman were of Americo-Liberian ancestry, some Americo-Liberians joined the secret indigenous societies, the same way some indigenous people were allowed to join the fraternal organizations like the Masons, etc. The Poros and Sande activities, which date back as far as the eighteenth century, are credited with keeping some likeness of order in times of social unrest, resulting in the membership garnering more power than even the indigenous elders or chiefs. One of the reasons that Liberia was able to resist colonization attempts was due to the secretive nature of these societies. Technically, Liberia as a country was not colonized by any country—not even the United States—although the US government played a major and an indirect role. The American Colonization Society was not a country but a philanthropic organization. If a person was caught revealing the secrets to an outsider, the punishment would rage from dismissal to death.

Traditionally, in the tribal areas, when young people reached adolescence, they were indoctrinated into what was called "bush schools," where they were initiated into adulthood and taught tribal values and traditions. The bush schools were run by the secret societies. The young people also learned other skills they would need in adulthood. Every tribe was unique; depending on the ethnic group, the bush-school period might last anywhere from a few months to three years. Upon completion from the school, the young adults often entered the outside world covered in white body paint, believed to make them invisible to evil spirits.

Due to the secretive nature of the activities, there are no detailed accounts of the curriculum of the bush schools, except to say that tribal values and other essential skills were taught during this period. The elders and leaders of the secret societies had control over the information that these youngsters received.

Materials used by the elders could not, under any circumstances, be communicated to outsiders. Skills such as farming, construction of houses, tracking animals, shooting birds, and carrying out a number of adult economic activities were learned—and continue to be learned in this method—by the youngsters during this period of their lives.

Normally, the youngsters live apart from their homes in an environment that looks like a scouting camp during their period of "bush school," creating a sense of discipline for the youngsters in the absence of their immediate family members. The youngsters also engage in the store of knowledge about particular subjects of the group. That knowledge is communicated through a variety of ceremonies, as well as in the form of stories, myths, and riddles.

In the early years of Liberia, the Americo-Liberian settlers periodically encountered stiff resistance and, sometimes, violent opposition from the Africans who had been there since long before the arrival of the settlers. Due to the complex intertribal relationships and the cultural complexities within each clan, as well as between the indigenous clans and the new settlers who had assimilated to the ways of the European West, indigenous Africans were excluded from citizenship in the new republic until 1904.

The Liberian story is similar to the Native American story in the United States. Like the American Constitution, the first Liberian Constitution made no mention of the natives until 1980, when a bloody coup d'etat brought an end to the 130-year rule of the newcomers' True Whig Party—also known as the Grand Old Party or GOP. The True Whig Party dominated all sectors of Liberia from the country's independence in1847 until 1980.

The inequalities between the two groups were codified in legal statutes. Historian Nat Gararea Gbessagee, in his book *Who Are We?*, reports that in 1862, the Liberian Supreme Court ruled that the aborigines were nothing more than subjects of the state who were required to abide by the laws of the land, but they were not entitled to citizenship because they were incapable of understanding the workings of governments.

The Contrast

Despite the strange relationship between the Americo-Liberians and the Native Liberians, there were some among the Americo-Liberian community who felt such inequality against Native Liberians was unnecessary. Among these was President William David Coleman. In his inaugural address of 1900, the president played to the stereotype inherent in the Liberian Supreme Court ruling in this way:

> "I have not the least doubt that all intelligent citizens [Americo-Liberians] are desirous for the elevation of this class [Native Liberians] into complete citizenship, that the sooner the fall of the superstitious customs that now exist among them, the sooner the object will be attained. Therefore, it is quite natural to expect that the effect of our civilization and Christianity has been to break down these gree-grees and other heathenish beliefs of our native brethren; this effect is just what is rightly to be expected as a result of our contact with them."

No one would have imagined in 1900, when President Coleman expressed such concern about inequity, that Liberia would one day be a country where all its citizens are protected by the constitution. It also tells how far the "civilized world" has come from inhumanity to humanity, whether in the United States, Liberia, South Africa, or anywhere in the world.

A Period of Mass Migration

A few decades earlier, in 1849, Joseph Jenkins Roberts, the first president of Liberia, requested that the United States buy territories adjacent to Liberia, so that his country could police the west coast of Africa from Sierra Leone to Cape Palmas, thereby helping to end the international slave trade. His proposal was rejected; however, the US Congress did pass a law instructing the US president to send a naval fleet to the coast of West Africa to capture slave ships and resettle those Africans in bondage in Liberia.

The United States put this policy into motion and by 1867, two years after the US civil war and four years after the Emancipation Proclamation ended slavery in the United States, some fifty-seven hundred African Americans had been resettled in Liberia. In 1891, additional free blacks migrated to Liberia; this time through a Danish steamer. The *Horsa* departed Savannah, Georgia, with fifteen hundred African Americans to Liberia (Njoh, J. Spectrum Books Limited, 2007).

The Congo people, primarily consisting of Africans from Central Africa, what is now the Democratic Republic of Congo, and the Iboes people from the Pepper Coast, now the Federal Republic of Nigeria, arrived in Liberia with no material possessions and were given assistance as they were handed over to the Americo-Liberians. The local ethnic peoples from the areas were also helpful to these new arrivals. The American Colonization Society provided some assistance as well. Many of these Africans, sold into slavery, were kidnapped in their own homes and placed onboard by the Portuguese and Spanish slaveholders to be carried away to the Americas. The British and American warships, being world powers on the seas, took the responsibility to divert any ships with African slaves en route to the Americas. They were diverted and landed on the shores of what is now today Liberia. The diversion of these new arrivals continued until 1860.

Because these new arrivals from Central Africa (the Congo) and Nigeria were new to this part of Africa, as were the African Americans who had been settling there since 1821, both groups gravitated toward each other, settling in what is now Bushrod Island around the Vai Town area; a section of Monrovia.

The ACS, the mother organization that helped to establish Liberia, was also instrumental in the migration process; by the end of the decade, the ACS had relocated 1,162 African Americans to Liberia at a cost of $100,000. By 1850, the organization had spent $1,800,000 to ship 10,000 African Americans to Liberia. African-American emigration interest rose again after 1877 with the collapse of post-war reconstruction in the US South and the withdrawal of federal troops from the southern part of the United States. Federal troops had been positioned in the South to protect African Americans.

Immigrating to Liberia, especially for African Americans, was not always without problems. Many of the prospective settlers died en route. They succumbed to fevers, tuberculosis, pleurisy, and other lung diseases.

Certainly, a primary reason for African Americans to seek freedom through emigration was the perception that there was no other alternative to the hopeless situation they faced in North America. But perhaps more importantly, African Americans migrated to Liberia because Africa was the land of their ancestors.

Another reason was that the American Colonization Society, which sponsored the repatriation process, was paying for their passage. Most African Americans could scarcely have afforded it and would have remained in the United States had the organization *not* paid their way. So, whatever their motivations were, credit is due to the leadership of ACS and the United States Congress that authorized $100,000.00 to purchase land and arrange for settlement in the creation of an African colony. The ACS as an organization was not racist; there may be some members who might have such intentions by evident to their writings. At the end of the nineteenth century and the beginning of the twentieth, tens of thousands of people came from different parts of Africa and North America in search of a new home in Liberia.

More than eight of the sixteen tribes in Liberia had relatives in bordering states such as Ivory Coast, Guinea, and the Republic of Sierra Leone. As the nation became stable and prosperous, migration of these tribes increased as well. The Gio (Dan) and the Mano (Maa) influenced considerable migration from the Ivorian/Liberian and the Guinean/Liberian borders. The same dynamic existed between the Liberian and Sierra Leonean borders, where family members left clan villages to migrate to Liberia. In some cases, the same tribe existed in two countries. The Vai and the Gola had settlements in Sierra Leone and Liberia; the Mandingo, Lorma, and Kpele tribes lived in both Guinea and Liberia.

The migration process to Liberia is similar to the migration that took place in the United States of America. The United States is sometimes referred to as a *mozia,* or mosaic, of many different cultures coming together for the purpose of improving their standards of living.

Prominent Liberians

Many of the Americo-Liberians who migrated to Liberia during the middle part of the nineteenth century and the beginning of the twentieth century became prominent in the Liberian society.

The grandfather of future President William Tubman, Reverend Alexander Tubman, was a Methodist preacher. Alexander Tubman was a stonemason, a general in the Liberian army, and a Speaker of the Liberian House of Representatives. Alexander Tubman's parents, Sylvia and William Shadrach Tubman, were part of a group of sixty-nine freed slaves who were sent to Liberia by Sylvia Tubman of Frankfort, Kentucky, in 1844. They took the name Tubman after arriving in Liberia and also named their community Tubman Hill. President Tubman's mother, Elizabeth Rebecca Tubman, came from Atlanta, Georgia.

William Tubman was the second son and went to primary school in Harper, Liberia, then the Cape Palmas Seminary, and finally Harper County High School. He joined the True Whig Party (TWP), the dominant political party in 1878, where he began his career in politics. Tubman was appointed by President Edwin Barclay as Associate Justice of the Supreme Court of Liberia, a post he held until his election as president in 1943.

Another group of settlers that eventually rose to prominence was the family of future president William Richard Tolbert Jr., whose grandfather originated from Charleston, South Carolina. The Tolbert family arrived in Liberia in 1879. One of his parents' four children, William R. Tolbert Sr. had more than twenty of his own, making the Tolbert family one of the largest Americo-Liberian families in Liberia.

Other settlers, like the Neals and the Taylors, came from the Caribbean and elsewhere. The families of Clarence Simpson and J. Rural Grimes also from the United States, are a few more examples. J. Rural Grimes was President Tubman's longest serving secretary of state. The family of President Charles Dunbar King came from Sierra Leone, and many of the descendants of the captured slaves from the Congo who were brought to Liberia, because of the assimilation process, all rose to prominence in the Liberian society.

Migration to Liberia continued even in the middle of the twentieth century during President Tubman's administration, when his Open Door policy was introduced in 1944. With the coming of foreign investments to the country, people came from different parts of Africa and around the world in search of opportunities. Liberia became the center of a robust economy in West Africa. A modern city was built by Tubman, attracting to Monrovia many tourists who had heard of Africa's first independent republic. America increased its investments in Liberia during this period to counteract the spread of Communism on the continent. Liberia became the conduit between the West and the rest of colonial Africa.

At the end of World War II, Liberia became a place of refuge for many people of color fleeing from colonial Africa, the Caribbean, and the United States. Liberia also attracted young revolutionary leaders like Nelson Mandela of the African National Congress (ANC); Patrice Hemery Lumumba, the first Prime Minister of Belgian Congo; Jomo Kenyatta of Kenya; and many others who received support from the Liberian government to advance their liberation struggles. Many of these leaders looked to Liberia as an example for the rest of the continent.

The period of mass migration also took place locally. Many of the indigenous Liberians began to migrate to the capital and other major cities along the coast. Another of President Tubman's policies, Unification and Integration, broke down more barriers among indigenous Liberians and new settlers.

Many of the indigenous people continued to migrate into the cities for better opportunities and education. This part of the Liberian story is similar to the northward movement of African Americans after the US Civil War and again during the Civil Rights era. This movement of people gives rise to the third category of *Congo,* known in the Liberian society as *civilized native.* Because of the complexity of the diversity in the Liberian society, one can hardly tell who is the actual Congo (or Americo-Liberian) now and who is not.

Migration throughout the world has one common factor: to improve one's standard of living. Due to lack of racial differences between the Congos (Americo-Liberians) and the indigenous groups, an individual can pass into the Congo group through adoption, wardship, and the informal polygamy relationship, an African system that allows a man to marry more than one wife.

Indigenous people also adapted the Americo-Liberian lifestyle or culture through apprenticeship, where native children from the hinterland were brought into the homes of the Americo-Liberian settler families. Within a generation, those adopted children had become assimilated into the Americo-Liberian culture so completely, they had forgotten their tribal origins and names and often their native languages as well. In most cases, these children took the names of the settlers—a similar indoctrination process as that subjected to Africans in the American slave period, as well as to Native Americans up through the 1970s.

Relations between America-Liberians and the Indigenes

From the beginning of the establishment of Liberia in 1822, when the settlers arrived on the African coast, America-Liberians presided over the development of a social system in which they assumed a significant superiority over the tribal peoples. In general, America-Liberians constituted a set of people who were creating social boundaries that were permeable only on the initiative of members of the set; paraphrasing in this context.

The social, political, and economic difference between these two groups of people were primarily based on values and ways of life. The settlers from the New World and their descendents practiced a completely different culture from the indigenous African peoples. Their system was totally rooted in American customs and traditions and vastly opposed to those of the tribal Africans whom they met in the area. The relationship between them was obviously tense.

Situations between the two groups began to improve during President Tubman's administration with the Open Door and the Unification Integration policies. Prior to that time, the America-Liberian population did not achieve a sustained interest in developing relationships with the tribal populations beyond what was essential and necessary to obtain needed domestic labor and maintain public order. An example can be seen in their different perspectives on national development projects like roads construction, public schools, and communication.

Issues like these and other types of inequalities were the major concerns of the indigenous populations. The tribal Africans saw such inadequacies as barriers that limited their acquaintance and social interaction with America-Liberians, who for the most part lived in the coastal region of the country while the tribal peoples lived in the hinterland.

Economic differences between America-Liberians and tribal people lay somewhat in occupational and income disparities amongst the Liberian society. America-Liberians were involved in a market economy as well as having access to the lifestyles connected to it. Most of the tribal people, on the other hand, were active primarily in a subsistence economy, specifically, subsistence farming, though some participated in a limited form of market economy.

Chapter Four

Making the Social and Cultural Connections

One cannot talk about cultural, social, and political connections between the United States and Liberia without mentioning the commonality between African Americans and Americo-Liberians, two groups of people that primarily and fundamentally show an appreciation for Western values.

History recalls that at the end of the slave trade in the United States in the nineteenth century, the freed slaves who remained in the United States went from "Colored" to "Negro," to "Afro-Americans," and finally, to "African- Americans". Meanwhile, the freed slaves who decided to return to their ancestral land called Liberia, were and are referred to as Americo-Liberians and also as Congo People.

In contemporary Liberian society, the phrase Congo People is used to describe anyone who is educated and lives a Westernized lifestyle like the Americo-Liberians. Many people who found themselves or who grew up in large urban areas in Liberia like Monrovia, Buchanan, and other coastal cities fall into this category, especially those who speak English and not any of the sixteen African languages of Liberia.

The Liberian story is very similar to the American story in so many respects. To be white in America is not necessarily the color of your skin or eyes, but can also be based on a mindset or a person's lifestyle. In the African American community, there is a phrase called "acting white," which simply means when a black person speaks like a white person or acts like one. Similarly, in Liberia, a person is considered "Congo", first and foremost because he or she is one or acts like one. That means the person's lifestyle is the same as a Congo person, or the person speaks like one. It is evident that there is a cultural connection between the two American-based African groups, even though they are two thousand miles apart.

Other types of connections between African Americans and Americo-Liberians are their names, religious practices, and the styles of infrastructure they brought with them. Hearing the last names of Americo-Liberians like —Dennis, Neal, Gibson, Anderson, Bernard, Brooks—and you hear very similar names to those that African-Americans inherited in the United States when their ancestors were taken to North America as slaves.

The settlers brought the architecture of Southern plantations and antebellum homes with them, many of which are still in evidence today. They built a number of cities along the coast and gave these cities Western names like New Georgia, Caldwell, Edina, Marshall, Millsburg, Bexley, Orange Grove, Virginia, White Plains, Bassa Cove, Carreysburg, Greensville, and Harper.

Other examples of the cultural and social connections between African Americans and Americo-Liberians are the religious and fraternal practices, how they engage in social activities, and their appreciation for the Western lifestyle, especially the English language. Marriage ceremonies are conducted the same way; so are family ties through names we call them—Cousin Joe; Uncle Ben; Auntie Bee, Sister Linda, and Brother David. This is how they establish social networks for opportunities in society.

In the Liberian society, it is called "Who Knows You?" You should be able to connect the dots to make your way. Like the United States of America, Liberia is predominantly a Christian nation, although, the Muslim population has grown in the last decades due to migration from neighboring countries and natural growth. It is fair to argue that Liberia is still America's "Footprint in Africa" because of those cultural and social connections.

We have power structure as connected to fraternal orders like the Free Masons and the Masonic Lodge of Liberia, founded in 1867, which encompassed seventeen subordinate lodges in the mid 1970s.

Two political parties existed among the Americo-Liberians: the Republican Party, which was comprised of "light-skinned" Americo-Liberians; and the True Whig Party, which was comprised mostly of "dark-skinned" Americo-Liberians. Prior to the 1980 coup, almost all important social and political leaders in Liberia and officials of the only ruling party, the True Whig Party, were members of the Masons. Many of these officials held high office in the Monrovia chapter known as Grand Lodge. Important policy decisions regarding national issues were made in the confines of the Masonic Lodge—usually a major contributor to resentment on the part of those who are not members of such an organization. Oftentimes, these nonmembers are from the tribal backgrounds with little or no connections with such people. How then can they "get ahead"?

Other social and fraternal organizations are the Order of the Eastern Stars of Africa (the women's auxiliary to the Masons), the United Brothers of Friendship (UBF) and its female counterpart, (the Sisters of the Mysterious Ten), the Odd Fellows, and the International Order of Good Templars.

In addition to the above organizations listed, there are other social clubs and groups with more limited range such as the Crowds Crow 12, Crowd 13, Crowd 15, and Crowd 18. These groups were the outgrowth of groups that had attended secondary school and university during or about the same time and have maintained their friendships in that semiformal status known as the "old-boy networks."

Activities in organizations like these are commonly practiced by African Americans and others in the United States as well. These kinds of organizations served as a conduit in Liberian society; climbing up the social echelon in society is made easier by participation in these groups.

Other types of connections between African Americans and Americo-Liberians are their styles of dressing both in social and church gatherings, some of the food they eat like collard greens, potato greens, etc., and how they set their dining tables; emanating from the American experiences the Americo-Liberians took with them to Africa. Liberia, like the United States, is a nation with many cultures and traditions; each with its own characteristics. Unlike the United States, there is no one mainstream or popular culture to dominated the rest.

When it comes to religious practices, Christianity is still predominant, although the Islamic religion is becoming increasingly noticeable. Like the African-American community, Americo-Liberians usually use the words "sister" and "brother" before the first name, especially in church settings and fraternal organizations, as a sign of oneness and love, an idea that is rooted in the African culture of brotherhood and sisterhood.

Other cultures carried to Africa by the Americo-Liberians were the use of outdoor toilets, raising chickens, and calling them with a special sound of voice: chie-chie-chie—, boiling greens, and having family reunions, all of which continue to be practiced by African Americans, particularly in the southern part of the United States.

One might think that African music would dominate the social life of Liberians. But there is great appreciation for American music, especially jazz and pop songs in Liberia. If a new release comes up in the United States, the next month, that song or music will be in Liberia. Liberian radio stations play American music about 95 percent of the time. That is one of the reasons why the rest of Africa considers Liberia "Little America in Africa."

Unique and distinguishable in Liberia's cultural connections to the American South were their dress code of tail coats, top hats, and cassocks, as well as the firm handshake and social kissing in greetings. Liberian men rarely embrace each other or kiss on both cheeks as they do elsewhere in Africa.

The settlers also took with them cultural and religious celebrations practiced in the United States; for example, the following days are observed in the United States:

Thanksgiving
Christmas
New Year's Day
Decoration Day (Memorial Day)
Valentines Day

In Liberia, the following days are observed as national holidays:

New Year's Day	January 1
Armed forces Day	February 11
Decoration Day (Memorial Day)	Second Wednesday in March
J. J. Roberts' birthday (first president)	March 15
National Unification Day	May 14
Independence Day	July 26
Thanksgiving Day	First Thursday in November
President William V. S. Tubman's birthday	November 29
Christmas Day	December 25

Ebonics

Another connection between African Americans (particularly Southern blacks) and Americo-Liberians is their manner of speech, known as Ebonics in America. The term Ebonics was originally intended to refer to the language of all people descended from enslaved black Africans, particularly in West Africa, the Caribbean, and North America. Ebonics may be defined as "the linguistic and paralinguistic features . . . that include various idioms, patois, argots, idiolects, and social dialects of black people" (Wikipedia, the Free Encyclopedia, 2005).

The term became widely known in the United States in 1996 due to a controversy over its use by the Oakland school board in California and has been used most often to refer to African American vernacular English (distinctively nonstandard Black US English), asserting the independence of this form from standard US English. In Liberia, there are still people who speak like Southern blacks in the United States.

History will prove Black Entertainment Television (BET) founder, billionaire Robert Johnson, right for investing in Liberia and urging African Americans to consider Liberia home like the Jewish people considered the State of Israel their home—because of the historical connection.

Liberian English Characteristics

In the eyes of most Africans, Liberians are "little Americans" planted in Africa. Besides the cultural, social, and political connections, the official language is English. The term "Liberian English" refers to the varieties of English spoken in Liberia. According to research, there are three different varieties:

Standard Liberian English or Liberian Settler English;

Kru Pidgin English;

Vernacular Liberian English

Standard Liberian English

Standard Liberian English is spoken by people with formal education and those whose ancestors immigrated to Liberia in the nineteenth century. This variety of English is a transplanted variety of African American vernacular English. This type of English is most distinctive in Liberian settlements such as Louisiana, Lexington, Bluntsville, small communities upriver from Greenville in Sinoe County, Maryland County, and the coastal cities of Grand Bassa and Montserrado. According to 2008 National Population and Housing census statistics, approximately sixty-nine thousand people, or 2.5 percent of the population, speak Standard Liberian English as their first language.

The dialect is different from Standard American English as well as other West African variants in that the vowel system is more elaborate and uses more gliding monosyllabic speech sound that starts at or near the articulatory position for one vowel and moves to or toward the position of another. Sentences and words are often not completed or spoken at all, deleting many consonants and verbs. Here are some examples:

He ain com yet. (He has not come yet.)

Am comin. (I am coming.)

Pas; Past.   (Don; Don't)

Haw (House)

Daw (Dog)

Seria (Serious)

Most of the time, the end consonants in multisyllabic words are deleted, as in the following phrases:

Re'li (Red light)

E'ry'thin (Everything)

Koo Aye (Kool-Aid)

Some words are used differently in Liberian English than most Americans usage. For example, *finish* means "to be out of something," as in "The rice is finished"; or *flog* is used instead of *beat*. Liberians also tend to finish many statements or words with a random *o*, as in "I am finished-o."

Despite of all the differences in pronunciation, Liberia is classified as an Anglophone country because English is the official language. However, English speakers who are unfamiliar with Liberian speech can find it difficult to understand children, adults with little education, or the many accents that result from sixteen other active languages as well as geographic differences. As in the United States and Britain, a Liberian person's accent can be linked to what part of the country he or she is from.

English is also spoken and written in standard form, that is, by international standards, by people with formal education or lifelong proximity to people with formal education. For example, people born and raised in Monrovia, the capital, speak Standard English, as in other large and relatively affluent cities.

Kru Pidgin English

The word *pidgin* refers to any kind of simplified speech used for communication between people of different languages. Kru Pidgin English is a declining variety historically spoken by *Krumen,* or those who worked as sailors on ships along the western coast of Africa, mostly from the Klao and Grebo tribes. These individuals also served as migrant workers and domestics in the former British colonies, such as the Gold Coast (present-day Ghana) and Nigeria. Their use of the English language would have been necessary to prepare them for whatever they needed to know to follow orders from their English-speaking bosses.

The tradition and language of the Krumen dates as far back as the eighteenth century. In the mid-twentieth century, the British colonial presence in West Africa ended. However, the ongoing use of the Kru Pidgin English continued along the west coast of Africa, including Liberia. Today, Kru Pidgin English—or non-standard English—is spoken by both educated and uneducated Liberians as an oral form only. Similar to Ebonics and sometimes referred to as street English, non-Liberians will doubtless have difficulty understanding many of the phrases or words. A few example of Ebonics, or "street" English versus Standard English, are as follows:

Standard: "Let's go for a ride, shall we."
Ebonics: "Hey baby, jump in ma low rider and rotate dees tires."

Standard: "Hello, sir."
Ebonics: "Whaddup!"

Standard: "Oh dear. What time is it at the current moment?"
Ebonics: Man, damn, what da time is?"

Vernacular Liberian English

Vernacular Liberian English is the most common dialect and is the Liberian version of West African Pidgin English, significantly influenced by the Americo-Liberian settlers. Its phonology also owes credit to the Liberian Niger-Congo languages, commonly known as Congo English.

The Vernacular Liberian English has been analyzed by experts to derive from a   post-Creole continuum. The post-Creole line of English is a range of dialects that extend from the highly pidginized to the common types of English spoken in Nigeria, some parts of Cameroon, Ghana, Sierra Leone, and the Gambia. Also call Local Varieties, Kru Pidgin is spoken by people with little or no formal schooling, particularly by people from the interior that speak English as a second language. Due to the Liberian Civil War, which began in the late1980s, most of the native people had to evacuate their homes for safety reasons, consequently finding no options but to communicate in English.

The Dominance of the English Language in Liberia

Why is English spoken so widely in Liberia? The answer to this question has to do with the history of the nation. One of the things the settlers did when they went to Liberia was discourage the speaking of tribal language in the settlements. That process continued with the arrival of Africans from the Congo and other parts of Africa. You would think that the African slaves that were diverted to Liberia would have retained their cultural identities. But they were discouraged from speaking their languages by the African American settlers; so that eventually tribal languages became seen as inferior to the English language.

Unlike other African countries like Nigeria, Ghana, Guinea, etc., where people are very nationalistic and take pride of their language and culture, speaking tribal languages is not a popular thing in Liberia. A person who speaks only his tribal language is often considered uncivilized or uneducated. Such practices have existed in Liberia for generations, so that even people from the same tribe tend to speak English to one another rather than speaking their mother tongue or primary language.

This dominance of the English language is also the American story, with a similar history of suppressing all other primary languages. Even with the significance of multiculturalism, a viewpoint that has swept American society in recent decades, English is still the dominant language.

The American experience has had a negative impact in the Liberian situation, as it has with other immigrant groups in the United States. Most children born to Liberian parents do not speak their parents' native language.

Even those parents who speak languages other than English as their primary languages do not take advantage of the opportunity to teach their young ones. The opposite is true with people from other parts of Africa. Many Africans from countries like Nigeria or Ghana with US-born children send their children home to learn their ancestral language and culture. In some cases, these children go through high school before returning to the United States.

Chapter Five

US–Liberian Relations in the Modern World

Liberia is sometimes called "America's Stepchild," a title from a PBS documentary. While it is true that the two countries have enjoyed more than a hundred years of friendship, there have been times when the relations took a strange turn. This chapter describes some of those challenges during the early years of US–Liberian relations, when the little West African nation was facing big European powers like Great Britain and France with boundary disputes, and between World War II through the Cold War in the mid 1900s, when the North American superpower was facing fierce opponents around the world.

Between 1871 and 1878, a prominent African American, James Milton Turner, served as United States envoy to Liberia. During his tenure, Ambassador Turner assisted the Liberian government in getting the United States to intervene in a conflict between the Liberian government and one of its indigenous people, the Grebo. It was known as the Liberian–Grebo War of 1876. Despite Ambassador Turner's effort to assist the Liberian people throughout his tenure in Liberia, he was not respected by the Liberian leaders.

One of the reasons for his mistreatment was because he was perceived by both sides of the Liberian political spectrum as interfering in the political battles between the Republican Party dominated by the Mulattos (known as biracial people in the States) and members of the True Whig Party, controlled by the so-named dark-skinned Liberians, who were in control of the government. In 1871, Ambassador Turner was accused by Liberian leaders of collaborating with the wife of President E. J. Roye in hiding stolen government funds allegedly misappropriated by the late president.

President Roye was called a *nigger* by Liberian opposition officials—all of whom were African Americans—verbally assaulting him as he attempted to carry out the instructions of the US State Department to collect debt that the Liberian government owed the American government.

Ambassador Turner was then forced to leave Liberia by officials turning the heat on him, because he opposed the concept of colonization in an article he wrote for an American newspaper. According to his biographer, Gary R. Kremer, James Milton Turner had successfully traced his ancestry to the Vai people of Liberia. He also discovered that he was related to Nat Turner, the African American who had led the bloody slave rebellion in Virginia in 1831 (1991).[1]

At the beginning of World War II, another African American, the honorable Lester A. Walton, born in St. Louis, Missouri, in 1882, was appointed United States Ambassador to Liberia from 1935 to 1946. It had become known as the Negro post, because Liberia and Haiti were the only two places where people of color in the United States held ambassadorial positions. Ambassador Walton was accredited to Liberia at the time when Liberia was facing one of the major political crises in the nation's history.

Five years earlier, Liberian president Charles D. B. King and his vice president had resigned, after an investigation of slavery and forced-labor charges by the League of Nations implicated the Liberian leaders. When the new president, Edwin Barclay, refused to implement measures recommended by the League of Nations, measures that could have compromised Liberia's independence, the Franklin D. Roosevelt administration refused to recognize the new Liberian government. But Lester Walton, the new ambassador, challenged FDR, pushing US recognition of Barclay's administration.

Lester also helped Liberia to obtain the assistance she needed from the US government to construct the Free Port of Monrovia, the first major port ever constructed in the country. Additionally, the ambassador presided over the Liberia–Pam Am contract, which eventually established the construction of Roberts Field (now Roberts International Air Port in Liberia). Ambassador Walton even went as far as advocating for the Liberian government by raising "the question of the restoration to Liberia,

---

1   Additional information about Minister Turner can be found is his dispatches to the US State Department, currently stored in the New York Public Library and the Library of Congress in Washington, DC.

[of] territories that Liberia lost to France . . . during the past century . . ." with the US State Department. Lester was also critical of corruption and human rights violations committed by officials of the Liberian government. He died in 1965. Ambassador Walton played a very important role in restoring Liberia's relations with the international community, especially the US government.

United States–Liberian Relations during World War II

US–Liberian relations in World War II comprised a number of motivations and pressures: (1) to finalize plans for the establishment of United States military bases in Liberia, which were to be used as a springboard to transport American soldiers, military hardware, and supplies to North Africa; and (2) to reaffirm Liberia's commitment to continue supplying the United States with natural rubber. (3) The United States and its allies wanted all German citizens in Liberia at that time expelled, because they posed a security threat to the United States and its allies; and (4) President Roosevelt wanted Liberia to renounce its neutrality and declare war on Germany and its Axis powers.

In *The Memoirs of Cordell Hull,* former secretary of state Cordell Hull, wrote, "With Japan's occupation of the rubber-producing areas in the Far East, Liberia became of greatly increased importance to us as one of the few remaining available sources of natural rubber" (1955), p. 1186). Thus was the purpose of Roosevelt's visit to Liberia in January 1943 obvious.

FDR insisted on going to Liberia despite the fact that he had a very bad cough and cold; in fact, his doctor had advised him not to make the trip. Besides Liberia's role as a source of natural rubber in the war effort, the Liberian territory was also used by the United States and Britain to ferry soldiers and military supplies from Parnamirim Field, the US air base in Natal, Brazil (now Augusto Severo International Airport), to the North Africa war theatre. You can see from the map on the following page that the route went from Miami, Florida, through Central America and Brazil, and then to the military depot at Roberts Field, Liberia, where five thousand African American troops were responsible for storing and maintaining the inventory.

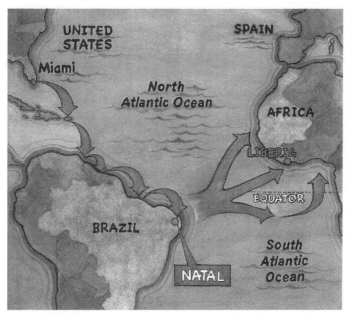

The transatlantic movement of US troops during World War II; (artwork by Bonita Geer)

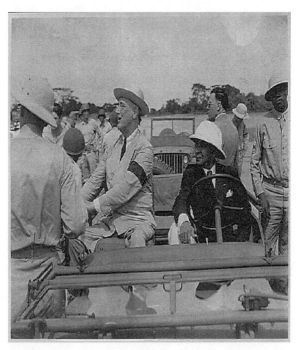

US President Franklin D. Roosevelt visiting African American troops in Liberia, 1943 (courtesy of the FDR Library).

From Roberts Field, the American war supplies were flown to three North African countries: Morocco, Tunisia, and Algeria. The use of the South American–Liberian corridor to transport American soldiers and war supplies to North Africa was crucial because German U-boats had taken complete control of the North Atlantic Ocean corridor and shipping had become unsafe for American war and merchant vessels.

The situation became even worse for the Allies after the fall of France in 1940 to the Nazis. Hundreds of Ally ships were sunk by German submarines in this region. Making matters worse, even the best military planes were unable to make the direct flight from the United States to North Africa. In General Eisenhower's "Crusade in Europe," the Liberian territory was seriously considered as the initial staging ground for the invasion of North Africa and Europe. The Liberian strategic location from Brazil and the North African war zone was so essential to the Allies that American and British military personnel almost came to blows—the United States military refused to let Britain fly its military supplies through Roberts Field. The situation became so tense that the matter had to be settled between Roosevelt and Britain's prime minister, Winston Churchill, at their meeting in Casablanca, Morocco.

FDR inspecting African American troops at Roberts field, Liberia, 1943
(Courtesy of the FDR's Library).

Between 1940 and 1945, rubber was to the United States what crude oil was in the 1970s—and perhaps even today. It was a scarce but essential resource and expensive. Scientific work on synthetic rubber was still at the experimental stage and not yet available widely. Meanwhile, Malaysia and Singapore, the major sources of the world's natural rubber supply, had been invaded by Japan, cutting that supply off to the West. Natural rubber was in high demand, especially at the peak of World War II, and Liberia was positioned to meet it.

It so happened that in the 1920s, as the US automobile industry was expanding, tire magnates Harvey Firestone and his wife, Idabelle, had been looking for a way to break the British monopoly on rubber. In 1929, they found an opportunity in Liberia, with its tropical rainforest suitable for rubber. The deal for Firestone Rubber Company (headquartered in Akron, Ohio) to operate in Liberia ended up involving W.E.B. DuBois, an African American intellectual who had taken a special interest in Liberia's welfare.

Dr. DuBois, a Harvard-trained social scientist, had visited Liberia in 1923 as US special envoy and regarded West Africa as his motherland. When DuBois heard that Firestone was interested in Liberian rubber, he took the initiative to speak on the country's behalf. DuBois wrote the Firestones a formal letter, encouraging them to pursue this interest, but at the same time, rather typically, lecturing them on the matter of trust—mutual respect and responsibility—it couldn't be business as usual, he said; exploitation should not be in the cards. Years later, the very thing that Dr. DuBois warned against had become the order of the day, by all evidence.

Firestone negotiated with the Liberian government a ninety-nine-year lease for up to one million acres, at six cents an acre. According to the agreement, any gold, diamonds, or other minerals found on the land belonged to the company. To be sure, the Firestone Corporation did make an agreement to loan the Liberian government funds for the development of its natural harbor—the Free Port of Monrovia—and made promises to develop Liberian infrastructure: for example, roads and bridges Akingbade, H. (1985) pp.25–36). At any rate, by the time World War II began, the Firestone Plantation was well underway, situating it perfectly for the United States, as far as the war effort was concerned.

The company, now the world's largest producer of rubber, is still operating in Liberia today.

Liberian Edwin J. Barclay with US President Franklin D. Roosevelt, (Courtesy of the FRD's Library) 1943.

FDR, the Tubman Administration, and World War II

President William V. S. Tubman took office January 27, 1944, ending President Edwin Barclay's fourteen years in office and Liberia's neutrality in the war. While Liberia's ally, the United States, had been using Roberts Field as a military base since the beginning, Tubman further aligned himself with the United States by officially entering World War II, one of the inaugural values of his foreign policy. The following June, Tubman and his predecessor traveled to the United States as guests of President Franklin D. Roosevelt at the White House, the first African heads of state to have been invited.

In the ensuing years, Tubman strengthened ties with his fellow African leaders by participating in the Asian–African conference in 1955, as well as the first Conference of Independent African States held in Accra, Ghana, facilitated by Dr. Kwame Nkrumah in 1958 (Dunn, E. (2009) p.12). President Tubman played a vital role in the realization of African solidarity and independence. In 1959, he sponsored the Sanniquellie Conference, which was attended by President Sekou Toure of the Republic of Guinea and Ghana's Prime Minister Dr. Kwame Nkrumah. The Sanniquellie

Conference was followed by another Conference of African Heads of States in the Liberian capital, Monrovia in May 1961. The creation of the Organization of African Unity (OAU) followed two years later in Addis Ababa, Ethiopia, by thirty-two African heads of state in the midst of the Congo crisis of May 1963. On the African continent, particularly in West Africa, President Tubman was counted by many Western leaders as a pro-Western influence. One of those Western leaders was President Lyndon B. Johnson of the United States, who had a close tie with Liberia during the Cold War.

Liberia's President William V. S. Tubman (courtesy of the US Library of Congress, 1944–1971).

President William V. S. Tubman: The Father of Modern Liberia

President William V. S. Tubman, known as "the father of modern Liberia," instituted his Open Door Policy to increase foreign investment; between 1943 when he took office till his death in 1971, Liberia enjoyed a period of prosperity. The Open Door policy also brought about an influx of people from different parts of Africa and around the world to Liberia. President Tubman's Unification and Integration Policy helped to unify and integrate Liberia, which had become a country of two separate peoples: one Westernized and the other Natives, commonly known as "country people."

Liberia was the only democratically free country, aside from Ethiopia during that period. The rest of the continent was still under European colonial control; up to the middle of the twentieth century when most of Africa gained independence. Tubman oversaw an unprecedented building boom. He turned the Liberian capital, Monrovia, into a modern city. The rest of Africa referred to Liberia as "Little America", even though Liberia was less developed than some African countries still under colonial powers, such as Nigeria, Ivory Coast, Kenya, and Senegal. Still, they admired Liberia as a symbol of freedom and liberty in Africa, despite her appreciation for the Western lifestyle.

Monrovia, the Liberian capital. (Courtesy of the National Archives Records, Monrovia, Liberia.) 2010

Chapter Six

The Cold War: A Period of Great Transformation in US–Liberian Relations

(L–R): President and Mrs. Tolbert with US President Richard M. Nixon. 1972
(Courtesy of Wikipedia, the Free Encyclopedia.)

The Presidency of William Richard Tolbert Jr.

William R. Tolbert Jr., who served as vice president for nineteen years, succeeded to the presidency after the death of President Tubman on July 23, 1971, in a London clinic. President Tolbert, an ordained Baptist preacher, inherited a country with a political culture dominated by the Americo-Liberians, who represented fewer than 10 percent of the population, and a modern economy overwhelmingly in the hands of foreign investors.

The tribal majority were basically excluded from both the Americo-Liberian–dominated political life and financial investment in the country. Tolbert put an emphasis on bringing the isolated interior into national political life and on improving the economic conditions of the indigenous population.

Having been in Tubman's shadow for nearly two decades, Tolbert surprised many and showed a dynamism in his leadership few people expected. Tolbert broke with Tubman's conservative formula, which was based on an appreciation of the West and in particular, of the United Sates. The second policy change in the Tolbert administration was in the area of foreign policy, which was totally contrary to Tubman's anti-communist doctrine. The third policy President Tolbert introduced, the concept of Humanistic Capitalism, was made in recognition of the fruit of foreign investments, which were unevenly divided, by gradually creating an avenue to renegotiate the concession agreements that had granted foreign investors important tax and other privileges.

Most analysts agree, however, that he will be best remembered for his policy of Total Involvement for Higher Heights, also known as Rally Time, which was aimed at improving the conditions of the majority of the people, starting with upgrading them from mats to mattresses. His was the creation of policies known as the Wholesome Functioning Society that committed the country to winning the war against ignorance, disease, and poverty.

Consequently, Tolbert's progressive ideas and policies were met with opposition, both at home within his own party and abroad. In 1979, his administration faced one of the country's major challenges when it was paralyzed by riots caused by a proposed increase in the price of rice, Liberia's primary staple food. The incident took the lives of more than forty people. The violence also affected many businesses in Monrovia, when demonstrators took to the streets of Monrovia and caused destruction in the business district.

On foreign policy, he committed to the Non-Aligned Movement, a group of nations with independent foreign policies not subject to east–west influence. The president based his foreign policy on the concept of Genuine Non-Alignment. In the heat of the Cold War, Liberia's relations with the United States began to take a downward turn. Liberians were awarded scholarships to study in the Soviet Union, Romania, and other Eastern Bloc states during the Tolbert administration, because he believed that a "hungry child cares less where his food comes," meaning it should not matter where help comes from. It was a policy that truly accentuated the values and principles of the Non-Aligned Movement. In 1974, Tolbert's administration accepted economic aid from the Union of Soviet Socialist Republic (USSR), and in 1978, Liberia joined with other developing countries in a trade agreement with the European Community.

The United States had supported Liberia with foreign aid because it was strategic as world war gave way to the Cold War. Liberia was considered an ideal post from which to fight the spread of communism throughout the rest of the continent of Africa. During the Tubman administration, the United States had signed a mutual defense pact with Liberia and built communication facilities to handle diplomatic and intelligence traffic to and from Africa to monitor broadcasts in the region and to relay the Voice of America (VOA) signal throughout Africa.

During President Kennedy's administration, the United States established the Peace Corps, as well as other economic and military assistance programs. Between 1962 and 1980, Liberia received $280 million in aid from the United States government, its highest level of aid per capita to any sub-Sahara African nation to date. In return for this assistance, Liberia had offered its land rent-free to US facilities. Liberia under President Tubman's administration voted with United States on most Cold War matters at the United Nations, consistently supporting the United States.

This support extended to the Vietnam War, when Liberia supported the position of the United Sates of stopping the spread of communism in Southeast Asia. Other US facilities on Liberian soil were the United States Aid for International Development (USAID) and the Omega Navigation Station, which monitors communications in the region.

All this changed during President Tolbert's tenure, when he began to welcome Soviet, Chinese, and Cuban ambassadors to Liberia in the promotion of Liberia's political independence.

Tolbert also weakened Liberia's relationship with Israel during the Yom Kippur War of 1973, siding with Egypt and Syria against Israel when he spoke out for the recognition of sovereignty of the Palestinian people at the United Nations General Assembly.

In 1978, US President Jimmy Carter visited Liberia, after initially planning only to fly over Liberia on his way to Nigeria. It was obvious that relationships between the United States and Liberia were not quite as tight as Liberians had thought—to have the first official visit by an American president to Liberia since FDR's stopover to visit US troops in 1943 only as an afterthought.

Carter spent only a few hours in Liberia before heading for Nigeria. Students from the Booker Washington Institute in Margibi County were selected to welcome President Carter at Robert's International Airport during those few hours. The selection of the institute was intentional—after all, it was established in honor of the prominent American Booker T. Washington, an African American scholar who had founded Tuskegee University in Alabama nearly a hundred years before. University of Liberia students were infuriated and felt what they sensed as President Carter's disrespect, given the long-standing historical relationship between the United States and Liberia, to have the American president spending just a few hours in Liberia, a President Carter at Roberts International Airport, while on a four-day visit to Nigeria. The short visit was symbolic, and not in the highest regard.

President Tolbert was assassinated on April 12, 1980, when seventeen young soldiers were led by an indigenous master sergeant, Samuel K. Doe. Also executed were many of the president's cabinet members and dozens of other government officials imprisoned. There is no evidence to suggest that President Carter's visit to Liberia a couple of years earlier has any connection to the assassination of President Tolbert in 1980. The visit was primarily intended to improve the already strange relationship between the two nations.

The US government supported the Doe administration, accepting him as a leader of indigenous origins who could finally open up the democratic process in Liberia to the entire population, and who would put an end to the political dominance by just 5 percent of the population. Doe became an important ally to the United States in the Cold War during the Reagan presidency. US–Liberian relations again took a positive direction, and Liberia served to protect important US facilities and investments once again. Liberia also assisted the United States in preventing the spread of Soviet influences in Africa. In the first five years of Doe's administration, the United States gave a large amount of financial assistance to Liberia: $500 million through direct and indirect assistance, the highest assistance ever given to Liberia by the US government.

President Reagan with Liberian head of state Samuel Doe at the White House
(Courtesy of Ronald Reagan Library) 1982.

In exchange, Doe agreed to do everything the United States had requested him to do. He granted the United States use of Liberia's ports to deploy a force trained to respond to security threats around the world. Doe also closed the Libyan mission in Monrovia and reduced the staff of the Soviet Embassy. In addition, he reestablished diplomatic relations with Israel. By the time the Liberian leader arrived at the White House in

August of 1982, the CIA task force had already pinpointed Liberia as a key operational and strategic area—an easily accessible base for the CIA's heightened clandestine campaign against Libya throughout the area.

According to US government officials involved in Liberia at the time, one of the first steps taken was to make high-tech improvements at one of the communication facilities in Monrovia. President Doe went as far as closing the Libyan People's Bureau in Monrovia in support of United States' interests. Liberia was also useful to the United Sates during a covert operation in support of Chadian leader Hissene Habre, who had successfully ousted his Libyan-backed rival, Goukouni Oueddei. According to Bob Woodward of the *Washington Post,* William J. Casey, a trusted adviser in Reagan's administration, had launched the Chadian operation after a national intelligence estimate he had read in his third day in office convinced him that Chad could be Qaddafi's Achilles' heel.

According to the *Washington Post* article (2005, p.5), the Reagan administration selected President Samuel Doe as one of twelve heads of state from around the world to receive support from a special security assistance program. Unknown to almost everyone else involved in making foreign policy decisions about Liberia in the Reagan administration, the advisers and foreign policy experts gave the CIA and the Reagan's White House a huge stake in keeping the Liberian regime in place. Relations between the two nations became even more strange toward the end of the Cold War in the Doe's administration. Corruption in the Liberian government was becoming an embarrassment to the US. The Reagan White House began to pressure Doe to return Liberia to civilian rule. The United States decided to cut off military assistance as well as reduce economic assistance to Liberia. It became obvious that things were changing once again between the two countries, with the cold reception given to US Secretary of State George Shultz by President Doe when Shultz visited Liberia in 1987. Doe was very upset, making the following statements to his guests:

> *I'm your best friend. I kicked out the Libyan Embassy that was here, and I supported you all over in the UN, and even in the Non-Alignment Movement. I'm always one of the three or four African countries that is on your side, and all the rest are against you. And what are you doing for me? You are cutting off our military assistance, and you are lowering our*

> *economic assistance. It's all one-sided now. I'm your*
> *friend, but you are not my friend anymore.* (p. 13.)

The argument by the United States was that there was no need or at least less need for Liberia's cooperation with the ending of the Cold War. The Doe's government was becoming an embarrassment to the United States; with major issues about accountability and transparency in the Liberian government. Coupled with the loss of support from Liberian society, the United States had no choice but to back off her assistance to his administration.

Chapter Seven

Cultural and Political Connections

An appreciation of Western life style by Liberians started with the foundation of the nation when the settlers from America first set foot on the continent. The Liberian culture is a mixture of both African culture, comprising 95 percent of the population, and the American culture that the settlers brought along. This is clearly reflected in the names of most of the cities that were built along the coast: Robertsport in Grand Cape Mount County; Monrovia, the capital of Liberia; Bensonsville, the capital of Montserrado County; Buchanan in Grand Bassa County; Greensville in Sinoe County, Philadelphia in Maryland County; Harper, also in Maryland County, to name a few. Ninety-eight percent of the streets in Monrovia are named after prominent Americans who were instrumental in the creation of Liberia.

The story of US–Liberian connection cannot be told without mentioning how the American story began. Some two hundred years before Liberia was created, a ship of settlers left England for the New World for two reasons: half of them were seeking political and religious freedom, and half of them were seeking a kind of financial freedom. Later, they became known collectively as Pilgrims and were followed by hordes of freedom seekers of all kinds. The irony is, it was not too long before the colony, and then the nation, found itself embroiled in conflicts around the freedom of the indigenous peoples they encountered there and that of the Africans imported as slaves—groups seen as having no rights to freedom.

Similarly too, the settlers who left the United States were primarily and fundamentally journeying in the name of liberty, for which the name Liberia stands, and then found themselves repeating the same contradictions as the United States had. In the case of Liberia, slavery was not the primary focus, but rather the disenfranchisement and exploitation of the indigenous population when it comes to national development. Like the Pilgrims that left England for the New World, the Liberian settlers brought with them the American experience of oppression. They thought of nothing but by dominating, exploiting and neglecting the indigenous people they encountered. Like the Pilgrims and the Indians, they had a very strange relationship for a number of years. The indigenous people were totally excluded from the political and decision-making process of the country. Even with assimilation of the indigenous people through marriage and trade, the Americo-Liberians still dominated the political machinery of the nation for more than 130 years.

At some point in the 1920s, the Liberian government was also found charging foreign users of Kru labor, which quickly became coerced labor in Fernando Po, Spain. The League of Nations produced a strong report written by Charles Spurgeon, an outstanding African American sociologist, criticizing the Liberian government for what was tantamount or equivalent to human trafficking and force labor. The League demanded that the practice cease, with pressure from the British and French governments calling for Liberia to be sanctioned.

So, it is fair to argue that the US/Liberian story is a human story: we tend to repeat our own mistakes, good or bad. One would think as the Pilgrims left England for the New World, as the freed slaves left the United States for Africa, the concepts of freedom and justice would be for all, but as humans (black or white), we are all subject to institutionalizing some form of inequality. Progress moves toward greater freedom, however, and relationships improved between the descendants of the indigenous and the newcomers over time.

Structure of Government

The United States declared her independence on July 4, 1776. Her "footprint in Africa," Liberia declared her independence on July 26, 1847, only seventy-one years later. The Liberian style of government and its constitution were fashioned on those of the United States. The United States and Liberia have the same three branches of government: the Executive, Judiciary, and the Legislative branches. The US Constitution stipulates that each state must elect two senators to the US Congress; similarly, the

Liberian Constitution stipulates that each county—equivalent to US states—must elect two senators to the national legislature.

The Americo-Liberian elites established a significant monopoly over the political structure and power. Like in the United States, the indigenous people's right to vote was denied for a very long time. It was not until the beginning of the twentieth century that the right to vote was granted to all citizens, enfranchising the indigenous population to full participation in the political process.

The Pledge and the Flag

Other similarities are the Pledge of Allegiance, which is modeled after the original US pledge (Liberia did not follow suit when the United States added "under God" in the 1950s).

The Liberian Pledge of Allegiance:	United States Pledge of Allegiance:
I pledge allegiance	I pledge allegiance
To the flag of	To the flag of the
Liberia	United States of America
And to the Republic	And to the Republic
For which it stands	For which it stands
One Nation	One Nation
Indivisible,	Under God,
With Liberty	Indivisible,
And Justice For All	With Liberty
	And Justice For All

The Liberian flag—the Lone Star—is also designed after the flag of the United States: red, white, and blue, except the Liberian flag has only one star, symbolizing the only independent republic at its inception, aside from the Ethiopian empire at the time.

The flag of the Republic of Liberia.

The flag of the Unites States of America.

Comparative Analysis: Contrasting the US and Liberian Constitutions

While it is true that the two constitutions had commonalities like the separation of powers, there are some differences if one looks closely. For example, the US Constitution contains much more detail about what the new state should look like, whereas Liberia's leaves a lot of questions unanswered.

One major unanswered question in the Liberian Constitution is what majority is required to pass a law, whereas the U.S. Constitution states a simple majority is required to pass a law for the first time; but to override the president's veto, it must be a two-third majority.

The Liberian Constitution also does not clearly define who can become representative. Neither does it forbid representatives to take other civil offices, nor does it promise that representatives will receive compensation for their jobs. Details about those aspects of the representation can be found in the US document.

At the time when the Liberian Constitution was written in 1847, there were only a couple of settlements on the tiny West African coast, with a total population of a little more than three thousand people. The Liberian framers were not particularly working with a mindset to present it as a democratic constitution. In contrast, the United States already had thirteen states and a large population along two thousand miles of coastline in 1787 when its constitution was framed, requiring more details for its document to be approved.

For example, the Council of Liberia (equivalent to the US Congress) was to be elected by Americo-Liberian men over twenty-one years of age, but the constitution did not prescribe how often those elections should take place.

One cannot deny the fact that the Liberian Constitution has roots in the US Constitution, particularly when looking at the people who designed it—all were members of the American Colonization Society (ACS), specifically, upper-class, patriotic, white Americans such as Bushrod Washington, the nephew of George Washington. These men literally copied the expressions of the US document when drafting the Liberian one.

It is very obvious that the content of both constitutions are related when one examines them. The Liberian Constitution stipulates that the American standards of weight, measure, and money were to be adopted in the Commonwealth of Liberia. Stemming from practical reasons for the times or not, the country was set up to be orientated toward the United States of America *by law.*

The Commonwealth of Liberia eventually became what is known today as the Republic of Liberia. The final major difference between the two constitutions is the issue of slavery, including slave trade, which is strictly prohibited in the Liberian Constitution. Obviously, the African American colonists had left the United States in order to escape from slavery. So in Liberia, their intention was to live as free people. Of course, this freedom did not extend to the indigenous African tribes that were living in the territories acquired by the Commonwealth of Liberia even before the arrival of the settlers. It could be noted that this was another similarity with the United States, which did not extend citizenship to the natives of North America.

To add to the complexity, as in most parts of Africa at the time, these different tribes sometimes fought each other. The captives from the battles were taken and sold on the slave market—contributing to the big slave trade during that time period. This practice became forbidden according to the constitution. However, natives convicted of crimes could be employed as forced labor (Dunn, Elwood D, et al. *Historical Dictionary of Liberia* (2001) p. 4).

In 1927, the League of Nations accused the Liberian government of recruiting and selling indigenous people as contract labor—slaves. In its 1930 report, the League admonished the Liberian government for "systematically . . . fostering and encouraging a policy of gross intimidation and suppression [for years]" in order to prevent the natives from realizing their powers and limitations, and to prevent them from asserting themselves in any way whatsoever, "for the benefit of the dominant and colonizing race ... [though] from the same Africans stock as themselves" (Dunn, Elwood D. et al.) Charles D. B. King, then president of Liberia, was forced to resign from office because of such practice.

A New Day

In 1984, Liberia broke ties with the United States and drafted a new constitution in Gbarnga, Bong County, Liberia. The commission, headed by Dr. Amos Sawyer, a political scientist from the University of Liberia, produced a totally new document with all new language. The new constitution accentuates the values and principles of the evolved Liberian people, including full representation. Like the rest of the new constitution, its preamble clearly epitomizes it.

Preamble of the new constitution

We the people of the Republic of Liberia:

Acknowledging our devout gratitude to God for our existence as a Free, Soverign and Independent State, and relying on His Divine Guidance for our survival as a Nation;

Realizing from many experiences during the course or our national existence which culminated in the Revolution of April 12, 1980, when our Constitution of July 26, 1847, was suspended, that all of our people, irrespective of history, tradition, creed, or ethnic background are of one common body politic;

Exercising our natural, inherent, and inalienable rights to establish a framework of government for the purpose of promoting unity, liberty, peace, stability, equality, justice, and human rights under the rule of law, with opportunities for political, social, moral, spiritual, and cultural advancement of our society, for ourselves and for our posterity; and

Having resolved to live in harmony, to practice, fraternal love, tolerance and understanding as a people and being fully mindful of our obligation to promote African unity and international peace and cooperation,

Do hereby solemnly make, establish, proclaim, and publish this Constitution for the governance of the Republic of Liberia.

Nonetheless, it is one thing to have a written document on paper and quite another to be accountable for implementing the values and principles of the document. Some may argue that the issue regarding lack of implementation of full participation is due to cultural difference or lack of understanding, rather than lack of accountability or intention. Whatever the cause, Liberia still needs to work hard to reduce the issue of implementation of public policy.

Significant Political Elements during and after the Establishment of the Commonwealth of Liberia

Liberia's first political party was formed in 1826 comprising mostly light-skinned, American-born blacks, commonly known as Mulattoes in Liberia or biracial in America. Originally called Independent Volunteer, the party later became the Republican Party. Another political party established during that period was the Anti-Administrative Party, which later became the True Whig Party, and is known as the Grand Old Party or GOP. This party was comprised of dark-skinned black Americans and native people. The GOP was the longest ruling party in Liberia, holding power for more than hundred years.

The political elements opposed the dictatorship of Governor Ashmun in 1828, who thought that the colonies did not have the intellectual power to lead themselves.

Monument of Joseph Jenkins Roberts, first president of the Republic of Liberia (Courtesy of Wikipedia, the Free Encyclopedia).

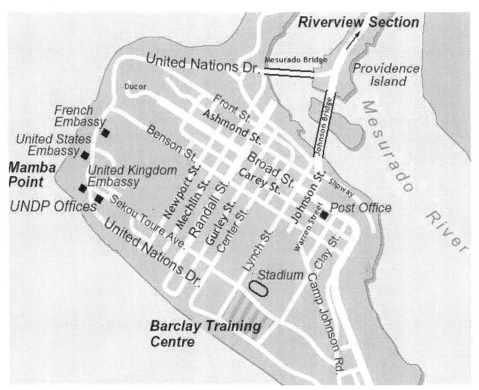

Map of downtown Monrovia, capital of Liberia;
(courtesy of TLC Africa, an internet magazine).

The Liberian Presidents

Between 1847 and 1904, 10 African-American served as presidents of Liberia; these were natural-born citizens from the United States of America. The following is a list of all the presidents of Liberia up to 1990. Some of these men served for shorter terms of office than others. Joseph Jinkins Roberts, for example, became president two different times. It is not clear what the term limits were during that period; or not officially honored. President William V. S. Tubman, one of the longest serving Liberian presidents served six consecutive terms and beyond, with a total of twenty-seven years in office. The new Liberian Constitution approved in 1984 set the term limits to six years for the presidency.

Joseph Jenkins Roberts was born in Virginia, USA, and became the first president of the Republic of Liberia at the age of thirty-nine. He served from 1847 to 1856. Roberts was reelected for a second term and served from 1872 to 1874.

Steven Allen Benson was born in Maryland, USA, and became president at the age of thirty-eight in 1856. He served until 1864.

Daniel Bashiel Warner was also born in Maryland, USA. Elected at the age of forty-eight, he served from 1864 to 1868.

James Spriggs Payne, born in Virginia, USA, was elected president at the age of forty-three. He served from 1868 to 1870 and was later reelected in 1876.

Edward James Roye was born in Ohio, USA. Roye became president at the age of fifty-four and served from 1870 to 1871. He was the first president to be deposed and assassinated in a coup d'etat.

James Skivring Smith, born in South Carolina, USA, may have completed Roye's term as president. He served from 1871 to 1872.

Joseph Jenkins Roberts was elected for the second time, serving from 1872 to 1876.

James Spriggs Payne served a second term as president from 1876 to 1878.

Anthony William Gardiner was born in Virginia, USA, and served from 1878 to 1883. He was the first president to resign from office.

Alfred Francis Russell was born in Kentucky, USA; he completed Gardiner's term. Alfred Francis Russell was president from 1883 to 1884.

Hilary R. W. Johnson was born in Africa but to American parents and was elected president at age forty-five. He served from 1884 to 1892.

Joseph James Cheeseman was born in Edina, Grand Bassa County, Liberia, to Americo-Liberian parents. He was elected at the age of forty-eight and served from 1892 to 1896. Cheeseman was the first president to die in office from natural cause.

William David Coleman was born in Kentucky, USA. At age fifty, he completed Cheeseman's term and was reelected, serving from 1896 to 1900. Coleman resigned during his second term in office.

Garretson Wilmot Gibson, was born in Maryland, USA. He completed President William David Coleman's term. He was elected at the age of 68 and served from 1900 to 1904.

Arthur Barclay was born in Bridgetown, Barbados, in the British West Indies. He was elected at age fifty and served three terms from 1904 to 1912.

Daniel Edward Howard, born in Buchanan, Grand Bassa County, Liberia, to Americo-Liberian parents. He served two terms from 1912 to 1920.

Charles Dunbar Burgess King, born in Freetown, Sierra Leone. King was elected three times from 1920 to 1930. Due to scandal, he was forced out of office.

Edwin James Barclay, born in Brewersville, Montserrado County. He was the first president who served two terms from 1930 to 1944; it is not clear what the term limits were in the old Liberian Constitution.

William Vacanarat Shadrach Tubman, born in Harper, Maryland County, Liberia, served six terms from 1944 to 1971. Tubman was the longest serving president in the history of Liberia and the second to die in office.

William Richard Tolbert Jr., born in Bensonsville, Montserrado County, Liberia. Tolbert served from 1971 to 1980. He was the second president to be deposed and assassinated in a coup d'etat.

Samuel Kanyon Doe, born in Tuzon, Grand Gedeh County, Liberia. Doe was the first indigenous president, the first military head of state, and the third president to be assassinated. Doe served from 1980 to 1990.

Interim Presidents during the Civil Wars of 1989–2003

Amos Sawyer (November 1990–August 1993)

Bismarck Kuyon (August 1993–November 1993)

Philip Banks (November 1993–February 1994)

David Kpormakor (February 1994–September 1995)

Wilton Sankawulo (September 1995–September 1996)

Ruth Perry (September 1996–August 1997). The first female to be appointed head of state.

Charles Ghankay Taylor, born in Liberia to an Americo-Liberian father and a Gola mother. He was president of Liberia and served from 1997 to 2003; he was the fourth Liberian leader to resign in office.

Moses Blah, born in Toweh Town, Nimba County, Liberia. Blah was the second president from indigenous descent. He served from August–October 2003.

Charles Gyude Bryant, born in Maryland County, Liberia, was elected by representatives of faction groups (or political parties). He was a civil society advocate during the peace talks in Accra, Ghana, and served as president from October 14, 2003, to January 16, 2006.

Ellen Johnson Sirleaf, born in Monrovia, Liberia, is Liberia's first woman president and the first woman elected head of state in all of Africa. January 16, 2006, to present (2011 at this writing).

Chapter Eight

THE LIBERIAN CIVIL WAR: A Missed Opportunity for the United States

On December 24, 1989, two-dozen armed insurgents quietly crossed into Liberia from the Ivory Coast, an event that introduced a new and tragic phase in Liberian history. The insurgents were led by Charles Taylor, a forty-year-old former procurement clerk who had fled to the United States after being charged with the embezzlement of millions of dollars belonging to the Liberian government. Mr. Taylor had escaped from a Massachusetts jail where he had been detained while awaiting a hearing for his extradition to Liberia.

As the fighting escalated in early 1990, the (first) Bush administration was faced with a serious question. Western Europe and most of Africa looked to the United States to take the lead in seeking a peaceful resolution to the Liberian crisis, since the country's history bears an unmistakable made-in-America stamp, sometimes called America's stepchild. But senior Bush administration officials were determined to limit US involvement in what was viewed as a *brushfire,* rejecting the notion of inherent American interest or responsibility, now that a post–Cold War era was underway.

In the words of Brent Scowcroft, who was the national security advisor to President George H. W. Bush, in a 1993 interview after leaving office, "It was difficult to see how we could intervene without taking over and pacifying the country with a more-or-less permanent involvement of US forces." According to Mr. Scowcroft, the United States' attention was "dedicated toward other areas more involved in ending the Cold War; like the fall of communism in Eastern Europe and Iraq's invasion of Kuwait in

1990 were taking that attention. The result would be seen in the build up to war in the Persian Gulf. "You can only concentrate on so many things at once," Mr. Scowcroft said. But there was still a range of senior US officials that were focusing considerable attention on Africa's oldest republic.

According to an account by journalist Reed Kramer, in an article: A Casualty of the Cold War's End, (2000) p.5; Liberia was a regular item on the agenda of the Deputies Committee of the National Security Council—where most of the foreign policy problems were handled—during the crucial period of increasing carnage in the civil war in the mid-1990s. As the crisis got worse, the deputies dealt daily with Liberia and Kuwait, according to participants in the sessions.

The account by Kramer on US decision-making processes was drawn from some thirty interviews the author had with policymakers at all levels of government in Washington, DC, and abroad. Additional research on the US role in the Liberian Civil War was compiled from historical materials and public records. Critics of US involvement argued that the US government did not do enough to stop the civil war, which took the lives of close to two hundred and fifty thousand Liberians. The argument was that the US government could have intervened in the senseless war that lasted for fourteen years and displaced a million Liberians around the world, including the United States. The United States' limited role in the conflict was an expression of a policy of selective engagement, said Kramer. It wasn't for lack of resources or the military capability to contain the conflict. The United States as well as any nation will ask a question: what is the national security interest or significance for the United States in the conflict? Is it political, economic, or regional? Proponents of the policy of selective engagement would make such argument.

Certainly, every nation operates in its own national security interest. The United States is no exception. History will show that the United States has acted along that line since the beginning of the twentieth century—from the Truman and Eisenhower administrations when the policy of Containment was implemented to prevent the expansion of international communism and Soviet power. The policy was proven to be a versatile and protean doctrine by the United States. In the Middle East, the doctrine was applied as a rationale by the Eisenhower administration in 1957 to back conservative rulers like King Hussein of Jordan and Camille Chamoun of Lebanon, who were besieged by domestic opponents. At the end of the Cold War, the United States developed an over-arching bipartisan foreign policy in the Reagan, Bush, and Clinton administrations best described as Selective Engagement.

The doctrine was neither unilateral nor multilateral in definition or application. It was a concept applied with differing degrees of intensity depending on the issue, moment, and the president's personal preferences. The assumption in Liberia was the United States would bring an immediate end to the conflict. To the ordinary people in the streets of Monrovia and throughout Liberia, who saw the airlifting of US citizens and other Westerners from Liberia during the peak of the war, the argument about policy variability made no sense. To them, it was an opportunity the United States could have taken advantage of the situation by stopping the senseless war and sending a message to the world that America was capable of aiding her step child during trouble times. Assistance that was provided by the United States for the reconstruction of Liberia afterward might have been unnecessary if such action was taken.

Certainly if the United States wanted to show the world she still had her "Footprint in Africa," in the little nation she helped establish, early intervention would have been the better choice. The history between the two countries was more important to most people on the African continent than a policy difference. Apparently, not for the United States.

It is therefore fair to discuss how nations formulate their foreign policies. Most of the time, foreign policy decisions are designed to protect that nation's economic, military, and political interests. With regard to the United States, the officially stated goal of its foreign policy agenda is to create a more secure, democratic, and prosperous world for the benefit of the American people and the international community. The question remains: did the US response to the Liberian conflict meet these above goals?

Underpinning the policy of selective engagement is the precept that in defending democratic freedoms, protecting human rights, and encouraging free enterprise, there remains America's historical reluctance to be engaged abroad at all, unless an international situation directly challenges American national interest. What did the United States miss when determining whether the Liberian Civil War met those standards or principles?

Let's take a look at the four criteria in defining policy abroad:

Is there a sufficient moral imperative or strategic necessity that requires the protection of United States' national security interest?

What are the costs in American lives and will American physical involvement be for a limited period of time?

Are there potential allies—especially in the region of possible engagement—that would form a working coalition with Washington to share human, financial, and physical burdens?

Is there a viable exit strategy from the engagement that would leave the political environment at home and abroad more stable than prior to engagement?

In the 1980s, there was another US foreign policy implemented in the Ronald Reagan's administration called Constructive Engagement, which tended to do business even with countries that had a record of human rights abuses as long as that engagement benefitted US national security interests. An example is the refusal of Western countries, led by the United States, to interpret and implement the 1977 arms embargo against South Africa's apartheid government, which was established forcefully and effectively under the UN Security Council Resolution 418, U,S.J. &Vale, P. current affairs, (1985). Because of the policy of Constructive Engagement, the United States argued the gray areas, which allowed Eastern Bloc countries to continue to do business with South Africa, restricted sales notwithstanding, and South African government continues to maintain its military applications in the oil and nuclear industries.

Toward the end of the twentieth century, the United States implemented its policy of Selective Engagement during the George H.W. Bush, Bill Clinton, and George W. Bush administrations, which stated that the United States could not be the policeman for every trouble spot in the world. Instead, America would get involved only in issues that benefitted her national security significantly, with possible exceptions on humanitarian grounds, if limited commitment was possible. Given this policy, it becomes clearer why America's role in the Liberian conflict was limited: after the fall of the Soviet Union, Liberia was no longer a strategic location. The same argument could be made about not responding to the genocide in Rwanda during President Bill Clinton's administration when they failed to make a commitment to contain the violence in that country.

However, invoking the policy of Peace through Strength, implemented in the Reagan administration to deal with conflicts in other trouble spots around the world, one could argue that intervention on those grounds should have been used to resolve the Liberian civil crisis. Such an intervention would have saved thousands of lives and probably limited the time it took to end the Liberian Civil War.

Still, with Liberia having lost its status as a "strategic nation," the Liberian Civil War did not meet the standard to warrant committing America's young men and women to harm's way. Nonetheless, the United States was involved in the Liberian Civil War in other ways. For example, the United States government resettled more than 100,000 Liberian refugees in the United States, making life better for them during and after the civil war. This trend of re-settlement of Liberians in the United States continues to this day. The United States also remains in strong partnership with the Liberian government for economic assistance and the training and development of manpower.

The Libyan Factor

Libya's involvement in the Liberian Civil War was an act of revenge both at the United States and the administration of President Doe. The Libyan leader, Muammar al-Gaddafi, wanted to retaliate against the United States for creating an obstacle to Libya's effort to extend its influence across Africa, particularly in Liberia.

Just days after the 1980 coup, Libya had announced that it would recognize the new Doe regime, becoming the first African country to do so; it then moved quickly to establish diplomatic relations. But there was a major worry on the part of US officials about such a partnership between Liberia and Libya, not the least of which was Libya's close ties with the Soviet Union and her anti-Israeli sentiment. But more important to the United States was Libya's long record of providing financial assistance and sanctuary to a long list of terrorist organizations from the Abu Nidal group to the Irish Republican Army to the Marxist revolutionaries in Central America.

So when word got out to the US government that Samuel Doe had accepted an invitation from Gaddafi to visit Tripoli, Washington became uncomfortable. In the words of a senior cabinet minister, George Boley, during President Samuel Doe's administration, "We were barely settled when I started getting calls from the American embassy urging us to back off, distance ourselves from Libya," in an interview by Kenneth Noble, a *New York Times* national correspondent, in his article "The United States, Libya, and the Liberian Civil War," published in 1998. As a consequence,

Gaddafi welcomed anyone who sought assistance in overthrowing the regime of Samuel Doe.

The man whose fighters eventually succeeded in that objective was the American-educated warlord Charles Taylor. The victory of Charles Taylor in the Liberian Civil War completed a full circle of Gaddafi's role in the recent history of Liberia. According to Noble's interview, one of the longtime political activists who also trained in Libya, Samuel Dokie, described it this way: "Taylor is Gaddafi's surrogate," and his election is also "Gaddafi's biggest victory in Africa."

Liberia became the victim of Cold War politics when ideological differences created conflict between two foreign powers breeding violence—the United States pressuring Liberia to separate its ties with Libya, and Libya giving arms and money to Liberian dissident groups. The final straw came with the decision of Colonel Gaddafi's biggest recipient of generous gifts, Charles Taylor, to invade Liberia in December of 1989. As the African saying goes, "When two elephants fight, the grass and trees suffer." Such was the consequence of the Liberian Civil War.

Gabriel Bacchus Mathews, then foreign minister during the early days of the People's Redemption Council government, in an interview with Kenneth Noble, said, "We were having problems with cash flow to meet salaries for Christmas, and we realized that we weren't going to have money. . . . The Libyans had been pushing for Doe to make a visit, and they wanted to know what the problems were and how they could be helpful; in the end, we proceeded to go."

Kenneth Noble reported that the foreign minister told him that the US Assistant Secretary of State Richard Moose brought ten million dollars in cash to Liberia in 1980 to prevent then President Doe from seeking money from the Libyan government. The American intervention influenced Doe's decision to close down the Libyan embassy in Monrovia—the People's Bureau, as it is commonly called in Libya—and expelled its diplomats. One can see why Gaddafi would turn to revenge in the downfall of President Doe's regime.

The Libyan involvement in the Liberian Civil War could reap three benefits: retaliate against Doe, support international revolutionaries, and poke an eye out on the Americans.

Chapter Nine

Liberian Outlook

Geography and People

According to the 2008 national population and housing census, the nation of Liberia has a total population of 3.5 million people, slightly larger than the state of Ohio. The land area is forty-three thousand square miles, stretching along the coast from Maryland County on the Ivorian border to Grand Cape Mount County by Sierra Leone. There are sixteen official languages spoken by the indigenous people, but English is the official language of business. Most Liberians speak English, relatively spoken in three different dialects: Standard English, Pidgin English, and Kru Pidgin or Local Varieties, as described in chapters three and four.

Land area: 111,369 sq. km. (43,000 sq. mi), slightly larger than the state of Ohio (*Embassy of Liberia, UK*. Retrieved April 2008)

Literacy Rate: 20 percent (UNICEF, 2003)

Unemployment Rate: 80–83 percent unemployment (Embassy of Liberia, UK)

Liberian Food Staples

The Liberian Agricultural research institute in Suakoko, Bong County, in central Liberia, and the Liberian Product Marketing Corporation (LPMC) are instrumental in helping farmers with locally produced products. The country continues to make efforts to develop beyond subsistence farming into commercial farming. But there is still work to do in this area.

Liberians have acquired a special taste for the following: rice, dumboy, and fufu; the latter two are made from cassava root only grown in tropical climates. They also eat fish, lots greens: potato leaves or greens, palava leaves, and cassava leaves. Other types food eaten in Liberia are bitter ball, palm butter, beans, peas, and other vegetables. Palm butter, made from palm oil out of palm nuts is very popular. All of the food types mentioned above can be eaten separately and not just as condiments or ingredients in food.

Liberia also produces other types of foods for local use, such as bananas, citrus fruits, coconut, etc. Another essential part of the Liberian cuisine is sweet potatos,mangos, pineapples, plantains, yams, cocoyam, eddoes, farina, and several types of nuts and peanuts. Fish is the most common protein because seafood is cheaper than meat, but meat—especially dried meat—is used sparingly as flavoring for dishes. Rice with smoked fish, known as *dried rice,* is also widely consumed.

Rice is the primary food, and most people eat it on a daily basis. People eat rice for breakfast, lunch, and dinner. A Liberian can eat any other food, but if he has not eaten rice, he has not eaten—that's how dominant rice is in the Liberian diet. There are two types of rice in Liberia: homegrown rice, which is known as *country rice* and is produced by native farmers; and *pusava* or long-grain, American rice, which is imported.

Due to the natural growth of the population, Liberia's demand for imported rice has substantially increased by 26 percent in the last twenty-five years. Other factors that retard Liberia's attempt to convert from subsistence farming to commercial farming include climate, adaptation to agricultural technology, access to markets, gainful availability of credit, a reliable delivery system, topography, and in some cases, environmental concern for the soil.

By the time President William Tolbert succeeded the late President Tubman to the presidency in 1971, Liberia was importing 119,357 pounds of "Pusava" rice per year primarily from the United States and elsewhere around the world. When the military coup of 1980 occurred, Liberia's rice import rose to 190,692 pounds per year, an increase of 60 percent in the demand of imported rice over a decade. This trend continues to exist even today of Liberians dependence on imported rice. It is somewhat troubling for a country located in a tropical part of the world with tremendous rainforests. Liberia also imports other essential products like petroleum, clothing, and basic daily commodities.

Household Traditions

Traditionally, Liberians live a communal lifestyle, meaning they live collectively. Family members are likely to live with other members of immediate and extended family. The number of people living in a typical Liberian household may vary depending on the family. The higher a person's income is, the larger his or her household will tend to be, though not necessarily. How many live in a household is determined by many factors. Family members still live with other relatives even if the sole provider is unprepared financially, simply because it is a right thing to do to care for each other.

The average number of person in the household in Liberia; especially in the rural areas, is between four to five per family. It is also common for men to take on more than one wife—in such cases, there will be a significant increase in the size of that household! Men with more than one wife also tend to build houses for each one of their wives. This is a sign of wealth.

In the villages and most rural areas, houses are built with mud and zinc sheeting, normally on one level. In the urban areas, houses are built like anywhere in the West, with windows and multiple rooms, and some cases, more than one level. These Western-style buildings date back to 1821 when the settlers arrived in Liberia.

Gender Roles

The roles of men and women are usually distinct. Women are expected to handle all children and household duties. The kitchen is solely a female domain, and men are encouraged not to interfere. Previous studies showed that literacy rates among women were significantly lower than for men. However, in the urban areas where most women are earning incomes like men—due to their success in formal education—the roles are beginning to change.

In the Liberian society, it is still an expectation that men will provide for the family and serve as main breadwinners. By the same token, men also expect to make all major family decisions and provide the necessary financial support for the children's education and health needs. Because of all of the responsibilities, the man is considered head of the household. However, everyone knows decisions in the home are not made by the men alone; women are a major part of decisions in the family.

Children and Childcare

Childcare in the urban areas can be very expensive, especially when both parents are working. But in the rural areas, having more children can be beneficial because it helps to make a bigger workforce. The older children help to look after their siblings and also prepare food for the family while the parents are out working.

It is culturally normal for children to be disciplined by people from outside the family, because "it takes a village to raise a child" in the African culture, and Liberia is no exception. The African community is seen as the broader part of the family. As a result, any adult has the right to challenge a child for misconduct. Many African Americans remember this same experience when growing up, as well.

Physical punishment of children for misbehaving is acceptable in the Liberian society. Parents have the right to beat or whip a child as punishment for misbehavior.

Children usually live with their parents until they are financially independent. Some move out when they marry.

The Elderly

Elders are usually highly respected members of the community. Ranging from forty-five years old and up, "the elderly" are expected to provide personal guidance and offer advice and support to the younger ones, because they are in possession of more knowledge and wisdom. Whenever there is a dispute in the community or family, they will provide advice and resolve whatever issues are at hand.

The elderly are also cared for when they are no longer able to look after themselves. The elders also have the right to discipline any child in the community, not necessarily their biological child.

Marriage

In Liberian society, there is a variation in age when people can marry, depending on several factors including education, geography, and income. For example, educated people tend to get married later in life. People living in the rural areas—where there is little opportunity for education or independent incomes—may choose marriage much earlier.

It is legal in Liberia to marry at age eighteen, but it is common for girls to be *reserved* before that age through engagement or arrangements between two sets of parents; this type of arranged marriage is particularly common in the rural areas. Known as a traditional marriage, a price is paid—a dowry—to the parent of their fiancé, for taking their daughter into their household. It is not uncommon for girls to marry as young as fourteen or fifteen in the rural areas, sometimes before finishing high school.

In most cases, couples tend to live together before marriage, especially when they are not Christians. It is also very common for men to marry more than one wife, provided they can support the women. Another caveat to the marriage institution in Liberia is that divorce is neither common nor popular, so many women risk getting trapped in abusive relationships, especially after they have children.

Homosexuality is not legal in Liberia and generally is sort of non-existent in Liberian society. If a person is involved in a homosexual relationship, that person is isolated for bringing disgrace to his or her family and the community; but in a rapidly changing world, there is a possibility that such practices may become a way of life for some people.

The Arts

According to experts on Liberian history and research from *Wikipedia, the Free Encyclopedia,* Liberia is renowned for its many cultural artifacts like decorative and ornate masks, and woodcarvings of human and animal faces, artistic expressions that can also be seen in other parts of Africa. Most of the time, these sculptures are produced in the rural areas where woodcarving is influenced by the lifestyle in the area. Artists there are encouraged to show their strong appreciation for and connection to the people, animals, and objects sculpted; and to develop their skills of observation for great detail.

Because of the traditional and close relationship between Liberia and the United States, there is also a tradition of producing American-influenced quilts, brought to Liberia by the original Americo-Liberians, free and former US slaves. The early settlers brought with them their sewing and quilting skills at the beginning of the nineteenth century and some of their descendants maintain the tradition today.

The 1943 as well as the 2008 census indicated a variety of occupations thriving in Liberia, including hatter, milliner, seamstress, and tailor. Most secondary schools in Liberia such as Booker Washington Institute, Bromley Mission (for girls), W. V. S. Tubman High School, Rick Institute, etc, included home-economic skills in their curriculums. In 1957 and1958, Liberia hosted a National Fair that awarded various prizes for needle arts. At that National Fair, Liberians from many ethnic backgrounds made quilts.

Literature

In the past, Liberia was known by Western historians as a country without a written tradition until it was settled by African Americans in the nineteenth century. Such a charge is disputed by numerous Liberian authors who have contributed to literature throughout the years. Research by Roland T. Dempster (2009, p. 4), reports, "Liberian authors have written on folk art, ancient proverbs, everyday life in the countryside, city life, religion, and sometimes the observations of their own lives." They have also written on other subjects like culture, tradition, identity, human rights, equality, diversity within the Liberian society, and pan-Africanism.

Edward Wilmot Blyden is one of the most renowned nineteenth-century Liberian authors. Recent literature on Liberia considers him as a diplomat, educator, statesman, and a writer. He is considered one of the early fathers of Pan-Africanism, along with W.E.B. Du Bois and Marcus Garvey. Blyden, et al., focused their writings around the need for Africans to develop their own identity and to become culturally, spiritually, and politically aware of their own potential to preside over their own self-rule and disprove the notion of Africans as people without culture.

In the twentieth century and as recently as 2000, other authors have taken a much less political but more prominent role in their writings. Authors like Bai T. Moore, Roland T. Dempster, and Wilton G. S. Sankawulo have all concentrated their work (both fiction and non-fiction) on culture, tradition, and modernization of Liberian society. Bai T. Moore's novelette, *Murder in the Cassava Patch,* is frequently a required textbook for reading in many Liberian secondary schools.

Mr. Sankawulo, a politician and author, published several collections of poems and stories, which later became praised anthologies on Liberian folklore and wider African literary tradition as *More Modern African Stories.*

Wilton's most celebrated book is *Sundown at Dawn.* According to the book's publisher, Dusty Spark Publishing, it is considered "one of the literary achievements of postwar Liberia and contemporary Africa."

Music

While it is true that Liberian music is a part of the wider West African music heritage, the nation has its own ancient music and instruments. This is evident in every country in Africa. As one travels from country to country, there is a distinction between them.

In Liberia, there are many different types of drums played by traditional artists. Drums of all different sizes are the most widely used instruments in most social gatherings and ceremonies. These instruments are used for both official and non-official occasions—in weddings, baby christenings, church services, graduations, holidays, and marriage ceremonies.

Traditionally, music is a main highlight of the Liberian culture whenever foreign leaders are visiting. For younger Liberians, there is a deep appreciation for American music, which can be heard at parties and on the radio. People enjoy listening to jazz, funk, soul, R&B, traditional rhymes, rap, and new music style. There is also gospel music, which is becoming very popular.

Dance

"The uniqueness of the Liberian people is fascinating"; quoting a multitalented entertainer known as Nimba Bird, who is also a member of the Tlo Ker Mehn from Nimba County in northeastern Liberia, "Liberian art, music, dance, and storytelling is a lifestyle. They are sociological and cultural studies of Liberian people."

There is a wide range of indigenous dance movements and styles that have existed for centuries throughout the country. The unique dance steps among the various groups vary according to ethnicity, ranging from Kru dances, Vai dances, Kpelle dances, Bassa dances, Loma dances, Gio (Dan) dances, and so on. Dancing is a primary method for retelling each of the indigenous traditions and expressing the culture of each specific group. These dances are not confined to their physical expressions but include other cultural factors significant to each region. For example, masks.

Masks are worn in most Liberian dances. The masks are a symbolic connection to those that are living with the ancestral spirits and ancient deities. Secret societies like the Poro and Sande hold the meanings of these dance symbols and serve as an avenue to share them only under certain circumstances. That means if you are not a part of these societies, your chances of learning about the process are very slim.

Due to the amazing artistic skills and energy, as well as passion, demonstrated by the dancers, the dances can become very engaging. According to master dancer Jallah Kromah, "The best dancer is the one who can make the grass skirts fly to see what is underneath with velocity."

Like the acquired taste of foods that people in a given society share, dancing can also have a feeling or taste to it. If you are an American or from anywhere in the West, there is a feeling of disconnect, even if the process is explained to you by a person who is culturally competent.

Media & Communication

Over the past decades, Liberia has supported several newspapers, including the *Daily Talk,* the *Liberian Herald,* the *Analyst, Liberian Observer,* the *Inquirer,* etc. Most of the journalists from these organizations have received awards both nationally and internationally for their commitment to press freedom and for promoting democracy in post-war countries like Liberia and other trouble spots around the world.

There are several TV programs and radio stations that broadcast in the Liberian capital of Monrovia and other coastal cities and towns like Buchanan, Robertsport, and Greensville. Primarily television and radio offer the most accessible means of communication to the masses of Liberians. Some radio stations are jointly operated by the United Nations and community councils like UNMIL Radio, Radio ELWA, Truth Radio, Star Radio, and ELBC (which is government-operated through the Ministry of Information). These media outlets serve as conduits to connect rural and urban Liberia to community-based apprenticeship programs for young people. These stations have been used to promote peace and reconciliation among the people after many years of civil war.

Most of the popular radio stations (if not all) have their headquarters in Monrovia.

Socio-Political Construction and Stratification

Every society faces the issue of division between the "haves" and the "have-nots," and Liberia is no exception. In Liberia, like every other African societies, one is either rich or poor. In the middle, are those who can afford but not necessarily rich or poor; known as middle class in the United States.

Wealth in Africa, and specifically in Liberia, has two categories: those who have money through hard work or family inheritance, and those who have the wealth of status in the community—for example, those in government like cabinet ministers, senators, county superintendents, and other officials in government. Men who can afford to have many wives might be considered rich. A sense of prestige and entitlement can also be realized through education—often known as becoming "civilized," or *Kwi,* as the indigenous people say.

The Kwi status refers to one's ability to speak English properly, a nominal allegiance to Christianity, a degree of literacy (education), and an involvement with material wealth—and if I may add, how you treat people. In Liberia, being civilized is also distinguished by Western-style clothing, architecture of homes, and household furnishings.

Social stratification in Liberia also derives from a distinction between how people dress, especially women. There is a strong differentiator for native women who tend to wear what is known in Liberia as *lappa,* which is a reference to the two pieces of cloth (lappa) that constitute native female dress. The status division between the poor and the rich can be associated with native vs Western lifestyles and geographical location. Among women, geographical location of the country is clearly identifiable by their dress. Most people who are born or live in the big cities tend to dress in Western style, while the rural areas promote more of the native lifestyles. However, there are plenty of people who live in the rural areas that also dress in Western style and speak English, especially those who have been to school.

African Culture versus American Culture

Collectivist:	Individualist:
Extended Families	•Nuclear Families
Identity is based on social network.	•Identity is based on individual.
Children learn to think in terms of "we."	•Children learn to think in terms of "I."
High-context communication	•Low-context communication

Extended vs. Nuclear Families:

A nuclear family is a group consisting of a father, mother, and their children, who share living quarters. A nuclear family can have any number of children. Historical records indicate that it was not until the seventeenth and eighteenth centuries that the nuclear family became prevalent in the West especially in Western Europe. With the emergence of Proto-industrialization and early capitalism, the nuclear family became a financially viable social unit. Extended family, on the other hand, is a group consisting of kindred who do not necessarily belong to the same family (husband and wife) or could be many generations living under the same roof. People living together as an extended family occasionally feel a great security and belonging. This is one advantage of having an extended family over a nuclear family. The extended family contains more people who serve as resources during crises and provide more role models for behavior of values. In many cultures such as those in Southern Europeans, Asians, Middle Easterners, Africans, Latin Americans, and Pacific Islanders, extended families are the basic family unit. In these types of cultures, the value system is generally collectivistic.

Identity based on social network:

In a highly collectivistic culture like the African culture, group is the most important unit. There is absolute loyalty to group; therefore, decisions are based on what is best for the group. The expectation is that the group takes care of the individual; the "we mentality" dominates in this culture. Private life "invaded" by institution and organization to which one belongs.

Identity based on individual:

In a highly individualistic culture as in most Western cultures like the United States, the belief is that the individual is the most important unit. People take care of themselves (including immediate family only), and decisions are made based on individual needs with more emphasis on individual initiative and achievement. The "I mentality" dominates in this culture; and everyone has a right to a private life.

High-Context Versus Low-Context Communication

Context of communication has to do with the way people communicate with each other. Some cultures such as African cultures value a high-context communication style, while other cultures such as the Western and Asian cultures value a low-context communication style. In the high-context cultures, information is either in the physical context or internalized in the person. Behavior rules are implicit; in other words, the context is supposed to give you the cues you need to behave appropriately. In these cultures, members tend to use a more indirect style of communication. A few examples of societies that value this communication style include Japan, Korea, China, Hmong people, and many of the Latin American countries. Other societies that value high context communication styles are South-Sahara African cultures; especially West African cultures.

In low-context cultures, information is part of and conveyed through the verbal content of the communication. The rules and expectations are explained and discussed; individuals tend to prefer a more direct communication style. Example of countries that would prefer this communication style include the United States and most European countries. In the United States in particular, children begin to speak their minds at an early age; otherwise known as being assertive. This type of cultural difference sometimes caused problems for American educators in assessing foreign-born children. Lack of making proper eye contact by a foreign-born child may be misinterpreted as mental or behavioral problem by a special education teacher. In other cultures, especially African cultures, direct eye contact by a child when communicating with an adult is considered disrespectful.

In the United States, for example, it is very common for college students to receive a course syllabus at the beginning of the semester. In it, students find detailed information such as the course description and learning objectives. It is not uncommon for the syllabus to also provide the instructors' policies regarding attendance, course assignments, course preparation, how grades will be determined, and even the course schedule. The reason for all this is because in a low-context culture like that of the United States, expectations are often communicated directly to the individual. In a high-context culture, students may not necessarily be given all this information directly. As a student, it is your responsibility to find out what the rules and expectation are. As the world becomes more globalized, some of these cultural differences are gradually being eliminated.

Administrative Divisions of Liberia

The country is divided into fifteen counties; in each county, there is a subdivision of districts, further subdivided into chiefdoms or clans. Montserrado and Grand Bassa counties are the oldest, both founded in 1839 before the country's independence in 1847. Montserrado is the most populated county; it is where Monrovia, the nation's capital, is located. Monrovia is both the political and commercial capital of Liberia. Nimba County is the largest county in area and the second largest in population, according to the 2008 census. Below is a complete list of the counties, capitals, populations, areas, and dates of creation as of 2008 census.

	County	Capital	Population	Area	Date of Creation
1	Montserrado	Bensonsville	1, 144, 806	1, 909 sq km (737 sq mi)	1839
2	Grand Bassa	Buchanan	224, 839	7, 936 sq km (3, 064 sq mi)	1839
3	Sinoe	Greensville	104, 932	10, 337 sq km (3, 914 sq mi)	1843
4	Grand Cape Mount	Robertsport	129, 055	5, 162 sq km (1, 993 sq mi)	1844
5	Maryland	Harper	136, 404	2, 297 sq km (887 sq mi)	1857
6	Bong	Gbarnga	328, 919	772 sq km (3, 387 sq mi)	1964
7	Nimba	Sanniquellie	468, 088	11, 551 sq km (4, 460 sq mi)	1964
8	Grand Gedeh	Zwedru	126,146	10, 484 sq km (4, 048 sq mi)	1964
9	Lofa	Voinjama	270, 114	9, 982 sq km (3, 854 sq mi)	1964
10	Bomi	Tubmanburg	82, 036	1, 942 sq km (750 sq mi)	1984
11	Grand Kru	Barclayville	57, 106	3, 895 sq km (1, 504 sq mi)	1984
12	Margibi	Kakata	199, 689	2, 616 sq km (1, 010 sq mi)	1985
13	River Cess	River Cess	65, 862	5, 594 sq km (2, 160 sq mi)	1985
14	River Gee	Fish Town	67, 318	5, 113 sq km (1,974 sq mi)	2000
15	Gbarpolu	Bopulu	83, 758	9, 689 sq km (3, 741 sq mi)	2001

Political Map of Liberia

Liberia's Contributions to African Liberation Struggles

Since gaining her independence in 1847, Liberia has played a significant role in the liberation struggles of Africa and the pursuit of global peace and human development. As a founding member of the League of Nations after World War I to maintain peace, security, and promote human dignity, as well as her participation in the creation of the United Nations in World War II, Liberia has served as a model for the rest of the colonies in their fight for independence.

Many African leaders from these formal-colonial countries came to Liberia for support and advice. Liberia played a major role and became a champion for the cause of freedom in those territories occupied by

Britain, France, and other colonial powers that were against the wave of liberation movements sweeping across the continent in the 1960s. Liberia and Ethiopia, the only two independent nations at the time, fought side by side on behalf of many territories that were struggling to liberate themselves from colonial powers.

An example was the action taken by Liberia and Ethiopia in November 4, 1960, when the governments of Liberia and Ethiopia filed a case against South-West Africa (now present-day Namibia), challenging the validity of the mandate of then Apartheid South Africa to control South-West Africa.

The mandate had been established by the League of Nations, giving South Africa the right to manage the affairs of the former German colony. As a result of this mandate, South Africa virtually annexed South-West Africa and did not abide by the international principles over the management of the territory.

Liberia also took a leadership role in the creation of the Organization of African Unity (OAU). Now known as the African Union (AU), the organization was established in 1963 when thirty-two independent African states came together to develop unity and promote peace on the African continent at Addis Ababa, Ethiopia. Before this historic event, there were several preparation meetings building genuine hope and vision for African unity. One of those meetings took place in Sanniquellie, Nimba County, Liberia. Attending the meeting were President Seku Toure of Guinea; Dr. Kwame Nkrumah, the first prime minister of Ghana; and President William V.S. Tubman of Liberia. Dr. Kwame Nkrumah had originally advocated for a United States of Africa, meeting with King Hassan II of Morocco and other African leaders at Casablanca, but support fell short of a continental government.

The year 1961 was a period in which a rift between the Monrovia and Casablanca groups almost caused a permanent division on the continent. Credit is given to Ketema Yifru, the former Ethiopian foreign minister, who was an active participant in all the negotiations and meetings that finally led to the creation of the Organization of African Unity. Mr. Ketema also played a major role in the August 1963 Dakar Foreign Ministers conference. The question concerning the location of OAU's headquarters was once and for all resolved among the leaders. Dakar is the capital of Senegal where the question of OAU's headquarters was resolved.

In 1999, an institutional evolution occurred in the continent when the heads of states and governments of the OAU issued the Sirte Declaration calling for the establishment of an African Union (AU), with the goal of accelerating the process of integration in the continent, to enable the continental body to play its rightful role in the global economy, while at the same time addressing the multifaceted social, economic, and political problems in twenty-first century globalization. In July 1999, the AU assembly decided to convene an extraordinary session to expedite the process of economic and political integration in the continent. Between 1999 and 2002, four summits were held to officially launch the African Union:

In 1999, the Sirte Extraordinary Session was decided to establish an African Union.

In 2000, the Lome Summit adopted the constitutive Act of the Union.

In 2001, the Lusaka Summit drew the road map for the implementation of the African Union.

In 2002, the Durban Summit launched the African Union and convened the first Assembly of the Heads of States.

As a continental organization, the African Union focuses primarily on the promotion of peace, security, and stability on the continent as a requirement for the implementation of the development and integration agenda of the Union.

Chapter Ten

US Policies toward Africa

The Political Map of Africa

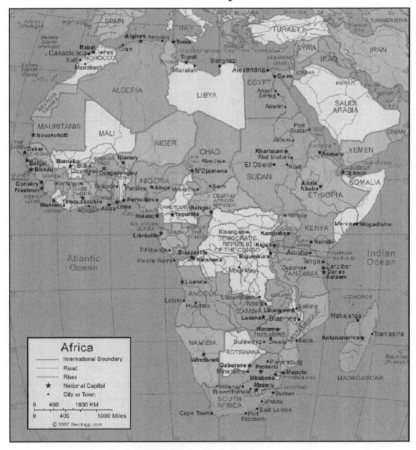

Courtesy of *TLC Africa Magazine,* 2009

As the old colonial powers (Great Britain, France, Portugal, and Belgium) retired from Africa toward the end of the Cold War, the United States began exerting its influence on the continent. America's influence can be seen in several African countries like Angola, Uganda, Ethiopia, Eritrea, Somalia, the Democratic Republic of Congo, and even obscure African countries that may not fit US national security interests.

In a 1998 investigation by Milan Vesely, et al., of neo-colonialism in Africa, the authors posed the question about whether the United States was Africa's new friend, whether she was playing "catch-up," or whether she was stumbling toward neocolonialism. The authors were wondering if an apparent diplomatic frenzy supported a coordinated US foreign policy agenda or if it was driven by economic objective—as the former colonial powers were, both when getting into the continent of Africa and when getting out.

In the past few years, there has been a signing of questionable mineral, communication, and financial deals by highly leveraged US corporations in different parts of Africa. Among these corporations are American Mineral Fields Corporation of Arkansas, in a billion-dollar mineral deal; New Millennium Investment, Inc., of Washington, signing a Congo telecommunications agreement; and the Leon Tempelsman & Son Investment Group, proposing an Angolan diamond operation. The Barrick Gold Corporation, a very influential US-Canadian mining conglomerate also announced an eighty-three thousand-sq km concession in the Congo's Kivu province.

Trade

The total trade between the United States and sub-Saharan Africa fell significantly in 2002, according to an advocacy group in Washington, DC. The two-way trade amounted to just under $24 billion—a reduction of 15 percent from previous years—US exports shrinking to $6 billion, while imports fell to $17.9 billion. According to the 2003 global trade record, Africa's share of total world trade stands at 1 percent, less than half of what it was in 1980. With the current global economic challenges, that statistic may even be less.

The African Growth and Opportunity Act of 2000 was intended to offer incentives to African countries to open their markets, but that law, approved by all member states, has brought very little benefit to few countries and has not resulted in sustainable economic development, especially in sub-Saharan Africa. In 2002, crude oil exported from Africa accounted for eleven billion dollars, or 61 percent of US oil imports from Africa; more important, oil imports from sub-Saharan Africa, especially Nigeria, along with five other nations in 2001 to the United States was 18 percent of total US oil imports, almost as much as she imports from Saudi Arabia. The National Intelligence Council projects United States' oil supplies from West Africa will increase to 25 percent by 2015, surpassing US oil imports from the entire Persian Gulf. Africa's Nigeria is the fifth largest supplier of oil to the United States, accounting for more than one tenth of total oil imports in the United States. Other major oil-producing countries in West Africa are Equatorial Guinea, Cameroon, Angola, Congo, and Gabon.

Aid

The United States still ranks low among all donor countries with about one-tenth of 1 percent of the GNP (or about ten billion dollars) going to foreign aid worldwide, one-hundredth of 1 percent, an equivalence of about a billion dollars, going to sub-Saharan Africa. However, in 2002, President Bush announced a new initiative called the Millennium Challenge Account (MCA). The five-billion dollar program was initiated to increase United States development assistance by 50 percent. The funds went to a number of countries around the world, including a few African countries that met specific criteria of good governance, investments in the well being of their people, and encouragement of economic freedom. The MCA was later changed to a new body called the Millennium Challenge Corporation (MCC). The MCC was a government-owned corporation, headed by a chief executive officer and employing both public and private sector staff. The MCC has a cabinet-level board chaired by the US secretary of state (from Wikipedia, The Free Encyclopedia, 2010).

Military Relations

The United States' military footprint in Africa has also grown in the last decades as her interests increase. US military bases and securing access to ports and airfields in Africa for strategic purposes can be seen throughout the continent. The United States has kept its main base for counterterrorist activities in Djibouti, East Africa, since September 2001. Another facility the US military has access to is Camp Lemonier, an ex-French military barracks located near Djibouti airport. The facility is home to eighteen hundred US troops. This base is strategically placed across the Red Sea from the Arabian peninsula. At one point, US Special Forces also trained seven-hundred-person rapid-development battalions in peacekeeping duties in Uganda, Zimbabwe, and Ethiopia. When asked if the US teams were a permanent fixture in Uganda, Rwanda, Ethiopia, and a half dozen other African countries, a Pentagon staffer once emphasized, on conditions of anonymity, "African governments recognize our military expertise."

A major concern in US policies toward Africa is her financial muscle, which has had a moderating impact on some African governments that maintain power through corruption, terror, and the subjugation of their own people. An example is America's thirty-year relationship with Joseph-Désiré Mobutu (Mobuto Sese Seko), lifelong ruler of Zaire. After Mobutu's death in 1997, that country—now the Republic of Congo—has experienced continuous social unrest.

According to Andrew Davison, a former British Foreign and Commonwealth Affairs official, "We don't seem to have much better luck—just look at how President Mwai Kibaki manipulated the elections in Kenya [and if I may add, the last elections that took thousands of Kenyans to the streets in protest]; President Robert Mugabe of Zimbabwe confiscating farmland; and President Chiluba's Zambian police shooting at his ex-president, Kenneth Kaunda."

US policy toward Africa must emphasize the importance of doing business with Africa. For too long, Africa has been the recipient of foreign assistance, be it toward farming, mitigating civil war, or in response to some other catastrophic situation. The questions for us now are these: Does Africa have anything to offer? Can something good come out of Africa?

Of course, the answer to both questions is *yes*. But it is a matter of having the political will to present the arguments among the continent's leaders and a real spirit of Pan-Africanism—not the nationalism that is based on putting one's own country over the others but a commitment to the entire continent. Such initiative can begin regionally; eventually, the rest of the continent will feel the impact and follow suit. This is very possible. There are resources available to make it happen—both human and natural—to make Africa a competitive partner to the rest of the world. That should be the mindset in post—Cold War twenty-first century Africa.

The United Sates is also promoting its troop presence in West Africa, a region that is strategically vital because of US oil interest. The little island of Sao Tome has offered to host a US naval base. During the George W. Bush administration, a one hundred-million-dollar initiative was created to support the counterterrorism efforts in East Africa.

More worrisome to US civil liberties groups is covert CIA involvement in destabilizing the Islamic fundamentalist government of the Sudan. Involvement in the internal affairs of African nations raises serious moral issues, argues Rev. Richard Rogers of the Southern Sudan Relief Committee. Over $20 million has been spent on the pretext that the rogue Khartoum regime sponsors international terrorism. Egyptian intelligence and an *Al-Sha'b* newspaper report states that up to 850 US military advisers are training guerrillas for the Southern People's Liberation Army (SPLA) of rebel John Garang. At the same time, US support for the situation in Sudan seems to lack clear direction, according to experts with authority on the topic. Ironically, the US-backed John Garang, on his visit to Egypt, made the remark, "We are not against Islam," contradicting the US view. At the same time, General Omar Hassan Al-Bashir continues to maintain control of Sudan, while the SPLA splinters into factions, some siding with Al-Bashir's administration.

During the Bush administration, economic sanctions were applied half-heartedly, mainly because of pressure from US corporations that depend on the Sudan's gum arabic (or gum acacia) exports for manufacturing. A Lebanese businessman critical of the situation asked the question, "Is this just another case of corporate America driving foreign policy instead of the other way around? Or is this an example of Constructive Engagement as in the case [of] US policy toward South Africa during the Reagan administration in the 1980s?"

Relief organizations were concerned by another trend: US oil and mining corporations that hire mercenary protection forces. Tensions between the local black-clad Cobra militia in Congo Brazzaville and ex-US military personnel guarding US oil facilities in Cabinda are already at a flashpoint. Those were the periods when US policies toward Africa had no real direction. As one relief worker asserts, "It is arrogant of these American corporations to have their own private armies on someone's national territory." Still, there seems to be no direction on the part of the US government. A Belgian diplomat was more authentic about the situation when he asked, "How long can this go on before a dozen US security [troops] are killed?" he wonders, recalling the deaths of thirty Belgian paratroopers in Kigali, Rwanda, in 1994. What will the US administration's reaction be, should this happen?

To many experts on US–Africa policies, this deep influence driven by business and military pressure constitutes a dangerous mix. On the other hand, there are others such as Rev. Jesse Jackson who had confidence in the process, according to the *Journal of Economic Perspectives* (1999), quoting the civil rights leader on US–Africa policies, especially on the Sudanese conflict. The continent of Africa and the United States have got a lot to offer each other, he predicted before his trip to meet then president of Kenya, Daniel R. Moi. The success of the sentiment expressed by Jackson hinged on three factors: corporate responsibility, a reduced US military presence, and a strong, clearly defined African policy on the issue.

During the Clinton administration, Secretary of State Madeleine Albright announced the US Partnership for Economic and Growth and Opportunity, which provided a $90 million loan to develop new oil fields in Angola. A subsequent statement made during a visit to a Chevron oil-drilling platform, when an additional $350 million from the US Export–Import bank was released to support the purchase of US equipment, got many policy experts concerned; it was a move that suggested that the state department was more interested in promoting US commercial interests than in African self-reliance.

In contrast, compare China's pending $150 million, no-strings-attached grant to the Congo. Critics will argue that the US requirements raise the specter of colonial thinking, even if that was not the original intent.

What is needed when it comes to US policy toward Africa, according to a relief worker, is a clearly defined US-government policy toward African governments to ensure that the potpourri of American big business, military adventurism, and interference in the internal affairs of African countries does not clash with the peasant population's aspirations. The consequences of not having a clearly defined policy will be far greater than the effects of Somalia, Liberia, or any other future trouble spots on the continent (Daniels, C. Mosaic African Studies E-Journal, Vol. 1 No., Howard University Press, 2010).

Africa's debt crisis

One of the major obstacles to development in sub-Saharan Africa, is the massive external burden of debt. African countries owe about $300 billion to rich creditor-governments and international financial institutions like the World Bank and the International Monetary Fund (IMF). Each year, African governments (especially in sub-Saharan Africa) are required to pay their foreign creditors about $15 billion in debt service. As a result, money is drained from other essential programs like health care, education, and response to the AIDS crisis, which is enemy number one in sub-Saharan Africa. It is important to note that most of Africa's debts are illegitimate, because they were incurred by African dictators during the Cold War and not used to benefit the African people. Some of the loans were given for failed projects that did not benefit anyone. The international debt relief framework known as the Heavily Indebted Poor Countries (HIPC) Initiative has failed to produce a solution to the debt crisis in Africa.

The HIPC was launched in 1996 and enhanced in 1999 by foreign debtors, but it has failed to reduce Africa's debt crisis to an acceptable level. Auditors from the World Bank have admitted that the HIPC initiative is not working. Interestingly, the United States is the single largest shareholder at the World Bank and the IMF, to whom most of Africa's debt is owed. So in fairness, the United States has the luxury to use her power to demand a new initiative to address Africa's debt crisis. For the purpose of equitability, an audit should be instituted of the debts currently being repaid by African countries, to establish what loans are being repaid and whether the debts are legitimate. Support from the United States in initiating such a proposal will be workable.

The AIDS Pandemic

This is one area where the United States has shown leadership, especially during George W. Bush's second administration, from the very beginning of his presidency. In 2001, the Bush White House established a cabinet-level council, chaired by his top foreign policy and health aides, then US Secretary of State Colin Powell and Secretary Tommy Thomson.

In May of the same year, the president gathered in the Rose Garden with UN Secretary General Kofi Annan and Nigerian President Olusegun Obassanjo to announce a maiden contribution of $200 million (subsequently increased to $500 million) during a new International AIDS fund launched known as the Global Fund to Fight AIDS, Tuberculosis, and Malaria. President Bush's financial contribution toward Africa represented a 30 percent increase over Bill Clinton's final budget in total foreign spending on the disease. According to a UN report on Africa, more than two million women with AIDS were giving birth each year, resulting in at least seven hundred thousand babies infected during pregnancy, during birth, or through breast feeding. Part of the reasons for such a high number of women was because they were unaware of any available treatment for the disease, and it was difficult to convince them to seek assistance.

Another initiative being supported by the United States is the program called the Mother and Child Prevention Initiative. The objective of the program is to increase the availability of preventive care, including drug treatments, and to devise delivery systems that would reach pregnant women and newborn children in two Caribbean and eight African nations.

When it comes to US policies toward Africa, particularly in fighting the AIDS pandemic, the Bush administration doubled America's financial support and efforts.

The foreign-policy objectives of the current Obama administration in Africa are rooted in four strategic principles: security, political, economic, and humanitarian interests. Testifying before the Senate Foreign Relations Committee, US Secretary of State Hillary Clinton told the committee members that the Obama administration's foreign objectives for Africa also included combating al-Qaida's efforts in seeking safe havens in failed states in the horn of Africa, and by so doing, helping African nations to conserve their natural resources and reap fair benefits from them. The policy is determined to stop the war in the Congo and work toward ending autocracy in Zimbabwe and human devastation in Darfur, in southern Sudan. The administration will support African democracies like South Africa and Ghana, two of Africa's post-Cold War democratic successes that just had their second peaceful changes of power in democratic elections.

Three hot spots in Africa—Darfur, Zimbabwe, and eastern Congo—are of great concern to the administration. The objective is to put together workable and available options. The situation in Darfur is a terrible humanitarian crisis, compounded by a corrupt and very cruel regime in Khartoum that president Obama will have to face during his presidency. The United States was supposed to bring the United Nations and the African Union with them in addressing the problems in Darfur. There is chaos in other parts of Africa as well, such as piracy, a flow from failed states such as Somalia and Zimbabwe (where the regime of Robert Mugabe has mistreated its own people), and violence in eastern Congo.

The twenty-first-century approach of US policy toward Africa:

United States' post-Cold War policy toward Africa in the Obama administration is based on mutual responsibility and mutual respect; that policy is focused on partnership; in other words, doing things with Africans, not for Africa. These are the sentiments that coincide with Africa's own growing emphasis on the core values of freedom, the rule of law and collective security, as embedded in the African Union's New Partnership for African Development (NEPAD). That effort to promote democracy and good governance are the mechanism reinforced by many African leaders. There are new strategic powers emerging in Sub-Saharan Africa like South Africa and Nigeria. These nations, in partnership with the United States, have used their diplomatic, economic, and military powers to shape the continent for the better. Nations like Mali, Mozambique, Liberia, Ghana, Botswana, Benin, and several other African nations are also leading the way as examples of the democratic rule of law. The United States has had success in working with its African partners to end major conflicts in places like the Democratic Republic of Congo, Sierra Leone, Ivory Coast, North-South Sudan, Ethiopia-Eritrea, and Angola. However, there is fragile peace in several parts of the continent like Darfur, Somalia, and Eastern Congo.

The new policy approach is grounded in the simple premise that the future of Africa is up to Africans. The United States will be a partner by providing security assistance programs that are critical in the process at three levels: (1) at the level of the African Union (2) at the sub-regional level and (3) at the level of individual states. At the level of the African Union, the United States is committed to supporting the Strategic Planning and management unit at AU headquarter in Addis Ababa with advisors and equipment; at the sub-regional level, the United States is committed to providing assistance to peacekeeping training centers in Senegal, Ghana, South Africa, Mali, and Kenya; and at the level of individual states, the United States is also providing peace and security advisors at ECOWAS' headquarters and continues to support the ECOWAS logistics facility in Freetown, Sierra Leone (Carter, P. III. Bureau of African Affairs, Washington DC, 2009).

Based on the premise of mutual responsibility and respect, a policy that has been initiated by the current administration, the United States is still committed to working with African nations to find solutions to the challenges facing the continent, especially Sub-Saharan African nations. In the Democratic Republic of Congo, Liberia, and southern Sudan, the United States is helping to rebuild professional military forces for those post-conflict states, and looking to engage in similar Security Sector Reform (SSR) activities in Somalia as soon as the situation will permit.

Chapter Eleven

Ellen Johnson-Sirleaf: Africa's First Female Head of State

President Ellen Johnson Sirleaf of Liberia

As they lined up to cast their ballots, thousands of excited women chanted and waved signs in the streets that read ELLEN—SHE'S OUR MAN, referring to Liberia's Iron Lady, Ellen Johnson-Sirleaf. Liberian women went out in throngs to cast their votes for this sixty-seven-year-old mother of four sons and grandmother of eight grandchildren who ran for president in Africa's oldest republic.

It is by no means an accident that this historic event happened in Liberia. After all, this is where it all began when it comes to democracy, freedom, and the quest for sovereignty in Africa. And it paid off as the announcement was made by the press that Johnson-Sirleaf had won almost 60 percent of the vote to become the first woman to be elected head of state on the continent of Africa. In a runoff election held on November 8, 2005, Johnson-Sirleaf defeated, by wide margin, Liberia's most famous citizen, George Weah, a millionaire soccer superstar. Weah got 40 percent of the vote. As expected in most elections in developing countries, Weah contested the election results, claiming that the election was fixed. However, international observers found no issues or anomalies to support that view.

Even though Johnson-Sirleaf is a tiny woman with eight grandchildren, her thirty-year career in government has earned her the title in Liberia and around the world as the "Iron Lady". A Harvard-trained economist, she has served as Liberia's finance minister and worked as an economist for the World Bank and the United Nations.

Mrs. Johnson-Sirleaf is also one of the few Liberians who has been imprisoned for political reasons. She was jailed twice for speaking out against past military regimes. According to Yassine Fall, a Senegalese economist who works for women's rights in Africa, "She is fearless! No men intimidate her," in an interview with the *New York Times* (2006).

Our Iron Lady insisted, however, in an interview with *Newsweek* that she wouldn't rule Liberia with an iron fist. She said, "In the past, I have been considered as one with a strong will, as a firm disciplinarian. But now, I'm most concerned with being a mother to Liberia. I want to heal the deep wounds of this nation."

No question, the country had many wounds when she took over in January of 2006, beginning on April 12, 1980, when a few enlisted men, led by the twenty-eight-year-old army master sergeant Samuel K. Doe overthrew the government of President William Richard Tolbert Jr., who was subsequently executed in his presidential mansion. For more than twenty-five years, the country has been torn apart by a series of conflicts, including fourteen years of civil war. Much of the country was in ruins from the fighting, which resulted in a lack of electricity and running water. Also destroyed from the fighting was the infrastructure of roads, bridges, utilities, educational institutions, and commerce, leaving an unemployment rate between 80 to 85 percent in its wake, according to recent reports on Liberia from UNICEF. President Johnson-Sirleaf also adds to the women's success story when she became the first female head of state in Africa to win the Nobel Peace Prize in October 7th, 2011. The 1.5 million honor was split three ways among Africa's first democratically elected female president, Madam Johnson Sirleaf; Ms Leymah Gbowee, a Liberian peace activist; and Ms Tawakul Karman, Yemen's "Mother of the Revolution" and a pro-democracy leading figure. The three women were recognized for their "non-violent" struggle for safety of women and for women's rights to full participation in peace building work.

Women are playing a major role in the government of Madam Johnson-Sirleaf, making up a third of her cabinet. Women have made several strides in African politics and cultures in contemporary times. In 2004, Kenyan environmentalist Wangari Muta Matthai won the Noble Peace Prize for her work in conservation. After the civil war in Rwanda, women occupied half the seats in the nation's parliament, more than any other African country. According to the Inter-Parliamentary Union, Africa leads among all developing countries in the percentage of women in legislative positions, about 16 percent.

Like the first black president of the United States, Barack Obama, Ellen Johnson-Sirleaf broke a historic barrier in Africa, and Liberia in particular, by becoming the first woman to be elected president on the continent. Since her election, Liberia has seen a dramatic turn-around in its economy, basic infrastructure, and educational system. President Sirleaf was inaugurated in January 2006, when Liberia's annual revenues were just eighty million dollars, about the size of a high school's budget in the United States. Given new government policies that encourage more efficient and ecologically sustainable exports of rubber, timber, and other natural resources, Liberia now earns $300 million a year in revenues. On the international scene, the president has dramatically reduced Liberia's once $4 billion debt to outside creditors.

In her campaign speeches, Mrs. Johnson-Sirleaf promised to have electricity in the capital city within six months. She also vowed to have a well or a pump in every village within two years. Her first concern was to clean up Liberia's corruption and reduce the debt-ridden government that she inherited.

"Our first priority is to get the government functioning properly and get our financial house in order," she said in an interview (allAfrica.com, February Edition, 2007). Her second biggest challenge was to respond to youths and their issues. The president wanted to make sure that there would be job training and schooling for the thousands of former soldiers. Education for young girls is another one of the major priorities on her agenda.

Liberia, according to the president, needs "a national identity, something everybody feels was necessary to bring the people together, that the nation has not had yet. We have always been America's stepchild, but never truly an African country, at the same time, never an American colony. We have got to find that thing that binds us," she said. National identity or nationalism has been one of the major issues among Liberians for generations. Unlike other African countries, where there is a strong spirit of nationalism among their citizens, Liberians have got to find that spirit that binds them together.

Ellen Johnson was born in Monrovia in 1938. She attended secondary school at the College of West Africa. After marrying her husband, James Sirleaf, she traveled to the United States to pursue further studies, earning a BA in accounting from the University of Wisconsin in 1964. Mrs. Johnson-Sirleaf also received a diploma at the University of Colorado in economics and a master's degree in public administration from Harvard University in 1971. During the 2005 elections, her supporters argued that she had two advantages over her opponent, George Weah: (a) she is better educated and more experienced (having held a string of international financial positions from minister of finance in William Tolbert's administration in the late 1970s after graduating at Harvard to Africa's director at the United Nations Development Programme), and (b) she is a woman making history. So, the question was, who is better prepared to rebuild Liberia's shattered economy?

After the 1980 military coup, Johnson-Sirleaf went into exile in Kenya, where she worked in the Nairobi office of Citibank. Five years later, she returned to Liberia to run for the senate and was briefly imprisoned for criticizing the administration of President Samuel Doe, and initially supporting rebel leader Charles Taylor. Johnson-Sirleaf moved back to the

United States from 1989 to 1996 when Liberia was entrenched in a civil war. In 1996, she returned to Liberia and ran against Charles Taylor in the 1997 presidential elections under the Unity Party, coming in second place against Taylor. Due to his insecurity, Taylor charged Johnson-Sirleaf with treason, but the resilient Johnson-Sirleaf campaigned for Taylor's removal from office, serving as the head of the Governance Reform Commission and assuming a leadership role in the transitional government after Liberia's second civil war ended in 2003.

In the private sector, the Liberian leader has also served on the advisory boards of the Modern African Growth and Investment Company (MAGIC), the Hong Kong Bank Group, the International Crisis Group, Songhai Financial Holdings, Women Waging Peace, and the Center for Africa's International Relations. Mrs. Johnson-Sirleaf was an initial member of the World Bank Council of African Advisors and a founder of Kormah Development and Investment Corporation.

According to recent reports, progress has been made in the following areas of the country by the Johnson-Sirleaf administration: in partnership with the US government, more than two thousand new soldiers have been trained, and the government has renovated the facilities at Camp Schieffin, as well as the Gbarnga military barracks. The economic growth rate has averaged over 6 percent in the past three years. Liberia is close to the end of the program that will bring the nation relief from the US $4.9 billion external debt the Johnson-Sirleaf administration inherited. Liberia's Central Bank international reserves have gone from US $5 million to US $50 million. The president has worked to remove the UN sanctions on Liberia's diamonds and forestry, joined the Kimberly process, (an international process to ensure trade in diamonds are not found in the hands of violence people or promoters of wars against legitimate governments); passed a new forestry law that is properly regulated, and joined the Executive Industries Transparency Initiative that covers or that encompasses both of these resources. On the educational front, enrollment in both primary and secondary schools has increased over 40 percent, the majority of whom are girls. The three rural teacher-training institutes have been renovated and graduated its first 456 students in twenty years. The University of Liberia is set to move to its US $20-million facilities to the new Fendall campus, about twenty-five miles outside of the capital. The Tubman Technical College, now renamed Tubman University, reopened its doors in September 2009, to be followed by the opening of another technical college in Singje. In the capital and a few other major cities, lights and water have been restored for the first time in fourteen years. On private investment, the government has attracted over US $8 billion in the nation's mineral, agriculture, forestry, and oil-exploration potential.

The government has also constructed and renovated more than 215 schools, thirty hospitals and clinics, several county administration buildings, courthouses, and security facilities throughout the country. For example, the Telewoyan Hospital in Voinjama, Lofa County has been renovated and is now in full operation, while a US $10-million hospital facility is undergoing renovation in Tappita, Lower Nimba County. Liberia has been qualified for the African Growth and Opportunity Act (AGOA) and obtained.

Threshold status under the Millennium Challenge Corporation. The president has strengthened the General Auditing Commission and established the Liberian Anti-Corruption Commission (LACC).

During the first three years of the Johnson-Sirleaf presidency, the Liberian government revenue has increased from US $80 million to more than US $347 million, pensions have risen from LD $50 to LD $1,000, civil servants salaries from US $15 per month to US $80 with a floor of US $100 per month for security, teachers, and health-care workers. Additionally, the John F. Kennedy Hospital has undertaken major renovations of both the physical plant and the building's capacity, moving down an irreversible path to recovery. Because of President Ellen Johnson-Sirleaf's efforts, the IMF and the World Bank have decided to support the final stage of debt relief for Liberia, which amounts to $4.6 billion in nominal terms. Liberia's recent graduation from the Heavily Indebted Poor Countries (HIPC) process brings the total number of countries reaching the HIPC completion point to twenty-nine, the stage at which full and irrevocable debt relief is said to have been won.

And finally, the president has restored Liberia's good relationship and reputation throughout the world. The fact is that there is still a lot to be done in Liberia and it will take some time for progress to reach its full potential in Liberia after the devastating fourteen years of civil war. But no one can deny that progress has been made in the past few years. President Sirleaf has begun the process; it is left with every Liberian and every friend of Liberia to make the effort for the mission to be accomplished.

President Ellen Johnson-Sirleaf with developer analyzing plans;
(courtesy of Wikipedia, the Free Encyclopedia).

Challenges Facing Johnson-Sirleaf's Presidency

Governance, whether in Liberia or anywhere else in the world, has it own challenges. The process involves making decisions that are sometimes unpopular with those it impact, and sometimes it is about the change—and let's face it, no one wants change. People usually like to remain in their comfort zones.

Among the biggest challenges facing the Liberian leader are security reform, which involves not just the police and military, but also demobilization, disarmament, and reintegration of former combatants, most of whom are young people with little or no education. While there has been some progress in this area, with more than seventy thousand combatants disarmed so far between 1998 and 2002 and more than 75 percent still applying to join the reintegration programs. Another challenge for the Sirleaf administration is making provisions for the return of seven hundred and fifty thousand displaced civilians, an effort that has been implemented with efficiency and speed. The reintegration programs also have a job-training and recruitment component for thousands of Liberians. The rebuilding of the army fell to the United States, while the UN is training the police. The US-led military reform project was outsourced to private contractors—DynCorp and Pacific Architects and Engineers. But due to a reported culturally insensitive approach in the implementation of the work, there has been some complication in the process.

Another issue that is facing the reform project is shortage of funding that has delayed the vetting and recruitment of new soldiers and reduced training on human rights issues and civil-military relations. The US government can be credited for deploying a number of Marine Corps advisors to step up the training process.

While the delays in the mission have presented a challenge, the final results have been generally satisfactory. According to a recent report by the International Crisis Group describing the army reform "a provisional success," more than two thousand Liberian privates have now being trained. Another challenge is the insufficiency of funds suffered by United Nations Mission in Liberia UNMIL, to undertake police reform. In addition, there are reports of flaws in the recruitment process and lack of momentum associated with the operation. The Liberian police force, with known serious corruption problems, is still engaged in deplorable and oftentimes criminal behavior, while remaining unable to address the worsening internal security issue in the capital and surrounding areas. Nonetheless, the dependable Emergency Response Unit, which has been a real success story, continues to maintain a thirteen-thousand-strong force and may even increase that number, because there is little incentive to intensify training efforts in the nation's police force. Some critics have argued that the president should be more actively involved in the reform process and other rule-of-law issues as part of her direct responsibilities, but unfortunately, that has not happened.

Judicial reform is another area still in need of progress—there have been a number of high-level cases in which the course of justice has been diverted from its intended purpose. Other judicial deficiencies include a limited number of trained, legal personal, a lack of infrastructure like roads, and bridges, and outdated rules of procedure.

The president has a lot of work ahead of her in this area if she is to successfully accentuate the rule of law in post-war Liberia. The rule of law is one of four pillars of the president's three-year poverty-reduction strategy.

The other three pillars are peace and security, governance, infrastructure and basic services, and economic revitalization.

While progress has been slow on rule issues, the Johnson-Sirleaf government has already made a substantial effort to deliver on her other campaign promises. Accordingly, in the 2008 Mo Ibrahim Index of African Governance, Liberia moved up six places between 2005 and 2006, placing it at thirty-eighth among other sub-Saharan countries, with a score of 48.7 out of 100. The area where Liberia has made progress most dramatically is the area of economic development. As might be expected of a Harvard-trained economist and former finance minister, Ellen Johnson-Sirleaf has proven to be more than instrumental.

The most conspicuous area of progress has been in the nation's natural resources development—fueled by foreign aid and investment, many companies have seen great opportunities. This area has been neglected during the Liberian fourteen years of civil war.

While it is fair to argue that Ellen Johnson-Sirleaf was the best person to lead Liberia at this time—given all the remarkable achievements as a stateswoman who has accomplished a great deal for the people of Liberia and continues to have considerable success in her administration—there are those who still wonder whether someone else could be doing a better job. How about someone with a totally different approach in policies implementation and governing style? Would someone with different orientations and leadership styles in governing take post-war Liberia in another direction to solve the twenty-first-century challenges?

Conclusion

It is my belief that when we educate a person, we educate a family; when we educate a family, we educate a community; when we educate a community, we educate a nation; and when we educate a nation, we educate the world. This is why I have written about the cultural, social, and political connections between the United States and the Republic of Liberia, a country the United States was instrumental in establishing. While it is true that the original American colonizationists and their supporters were more concerned about their own economic, political, and security interests than those of freed African Americans in the time before slavery was ended, the issue is moot. Their initiative created a place of freedom where freed slaves could re-pattern their lives in a new nation of their own.

This historical document also tried to lay out a detailed account of what it took the founders of this West African nation to reach success. Like the start of any initiative, there were difficulties, including opposition from indigenous and foreign powers. As a sovereign nation, Liberia continues to face many challenges, both internal and external, but the US government also continues to provide political, financial, humanitarian, and at some point, military support to what is considered her Footprint in Africa.

The Liberian society, like the United States, is comprised of many different peoples. Its significant cultural complexities presented challenges any new nation would hope not to face head on. Conflicts in value systems between the indigenous Africans and the freed American blacks and also with other Africans who were brought to Liberia by the US and British navies diverting slave-trading ships to her shores and freeing the illegally procured Africans on board. These three groups now live side-by-side, assimilated and integrated by education, commerce, marriage, and law after many years of indifference.

Even today, our culture has much that reflects its American roots. As African Americans have given much to the culture of the West, the West has given much of its culture to Liberia. I wanted to show some of the details of that—names of streets and cities, people's last names, architecture designs, music, the Liberian Constitution and Pledge of Allegiance, our structure of government, our religious and family values.

Certainly, there are issues regarding US–Liberian relations that were not addressed in this book; this was only an attempt to present an overview of our cultural, social, and political connections. My primary intention was to lay a chronological foundation of those events that led to the creation of Liberia, a nation called variously Little America and America's Stepchild, depending on who is doing the calling; the events that led to groundwork decisions made by the founding fathers; an introduction to the major players in the process; and an overview of the results of their decisions.

For more than a hundred and ninety four years, starting with that first meeting in 1816 in Washington, DC, America has been involved with Liberian affairs—directly or indirectly—from addressing boundary issues with the British and French in the 1820s–1830s and again in the 1920s when Liberia's sovereignty was nearly taken away over human rights abuses, to giving millions of dollars in loans during tough economic times; from underwriting the transportation of tens of thousands of African Americans long ago to resettle in Liberia, and in recent time, by resettling nearly hundred and fifty thousand Liberian refugees in the United States due to a fourteen-year civil war.

The relationship has had mutual benefit. A major portion of the book is focused on World War II and the Cold War politics, when Liberia was situated strategically for US military strength. FDR's visit to Liberia also served to show his administration's support of African-American troops during World War II. From President William Tubman and Samuel Doe with Ronald Reagan at the end of the Cold War, the US–Liberian relationship was a major part of America's foreign policy in Africa.

I have tried to offer a true sense of understanding, within a historical context, the long and close relationship between the United States of America and the Republic of Liberia. In a real sense, this book is both an African American and Liberian history. Therefore, it is an American history, because it accentuates the values and principles that were carried back to Africa by African Americans who were the founding fathers of Liberia. Not to put too soft a light on it, I did my best to include the underside of our histories as well—the less-than-stellar motivations of the committee that generated the colonization in the beginning, the oppression of the indigenous people by the Americo-Liberians, and the rich cultures that the sixteen African tribes had before the arrival of the Americo-Liberians and their crucial role in making freedom an authentic value in Liberian history.

The purpose for writing this book was to produce an account that depicts the true nature of US/Liberian history; a story that has not been told clearly enough on either side of the Atlantic.

ABOUT THE AUTHOR

JESSE MONGRUE IS AN EDUCATOR AND HISTORIAN ON US/ LIBERIA'S RELATIONS. JESSE AND HIS WIFE AUDREY DUNDAS MONGRUE ALONG WITH THEIR FOUR CHILDREN LIVE IN THE CITY OF VADNAIS HEIGHTS, A SUBURB OF SAINT PAUL, MINNESOTA. HE HOLDS A BACHELOR'S DEGREE IN PUBLIC ADMINISTRATION FROM LANGSTON UNIVERSITY IN OKLAHOMA AND A MASTERS DEGREE IN EDUCATIONAL ADMINISTRATION FROM SAINT MARY'S UNIVERSITY IN MINNESOTA. JESSE IS ALSO A HOWARD UNIVERSITY TRAINED POLICY ANALYST, WHO HAS DONE A NUMBER OF SCHOLARLY WORKS IN PUBLIC POLICY FOR SEVERAL AGENCIES INCLUDING THE OFFICE OF POLICY, US DEPARTMENT OF LABOR, NASA'S GODDARD SPACE FLIGHT CENTER IN GREENBELT, MARYLAND, AND THE OFFICE OF POLICY AND PLANNING, GOVERNMENT OF THE DISTRICT OF COLUMBIA.

THE AUTHOR IS AN AVID READER OF US/LIBERIA'S RELATIONS WITH EMPHASIS ON THE CULTURAL, SOCIAL, AND POLITICAL CONNECTIONS. JESSE MONGRUE IS A RECIPIENT OF SEVERAL DISTINGUISHED PUBLIC SERVICE AND PROFESSIONAL DEVELOPMENT AWARDS FROM NASA'S GODDARD SPACE FLIGHT CENTER, WILDER FOUNDATION, CITY OF DALLAS, AND DOZENS OF OTHER AGENCIES. HE WAS RECOGNIZED FOR OUTSTANDING LEADERSHIP IN THE LIBERIAN COMMUNITY IN MINNESOTA IN 2009. THE AUTHOR IS A MEMBER OF SEVERAL PROFESSIONAL ORGANIZATIONS INCLUDING THE NATIONAL FORUM FOR BLACK PUBLIC ADMINISTRATORS, PHI BETA SIGMA FRATERNITY, AND THE BOARD OF DIRECTORS OF NORTHWEST HENNEPIN FAMILY SERVICES COLLABORATIVE GOVERNANCE COMMISSION IN MINNESOTA.

Appendix

Important Events Before and After the Establishment of Liberia

AD 00–1100 The area to be known as Liberia is believed to be inhabited by the Kumba tribes (Kpelle, Loma, Gbande, and Mano (Maa).

700–1100 Ghana Empire (also known as Wangadou Empire): located in what is now Southeastern Mauritania and present day Mali was one of the oldest empires in West Africa.

800–1550 Mali Empire or (Mandingo Empire): rose to power and coexisted independently with Ghana and Songhai Empires for centuries.

1200 Arrival of Spanish explorers to the area one day to be known as Liberia.

1300–1600 Songhai Empire (or Songhay Empire) was the largest and greatest empire in West Africa.

1364–1413 Arrival of the Normans from France. French Normans establish the trading posts of Grand Dieppe and Petit Dieppe in the area.

1375 The powerful Mali Empire goes into decline, bringing rise to power of the Songhai Empire.

1461 Arrival of Portuguese explorers, led by Pedro de Sintra, who name the area the Grain Coast. During this time, the melegueta pepper, with seeds known as "grains of paradise," is one of the most valuable trade commodities for both its culinary and medical qualities. The Portuguese trade monopoly with tribes in West Africa lasts until 1515, and includes ivory and gold in addition to pepper grains and other spices. Nearly all the prominent capes, rivers, and islets off the coast of Liberia, especially in present-day Sinoe and Maryland counties still bear Portuguese names.

1500s The Kru, Bassa, Dei, Mamba, and Grebo tribes immigrate to the Grain Coast from an area known today as the Republic of Ivory Coast.

1500s Portuguese and British traders participated in the Transatlantic Slave Trade in this region. Historical records showed the Bassa, Kru, and Mende tribes as the primary participants in the slave trade in the area.

1591 Songhai Empire began its decline.

1600s Muslim tribes of Vai and Mandingo immigrate to the Western coast of Liberia from the Sudan. The Mandingo traders and artisans play a major role by becoming principal propagators of Islam as they spread their influence throughout the region. Besides the decline of the powerful Mali and Songhai empires, migrations to the region is also due to the favorable agricultural and economic conditions tied to the availability of fertile land in the area.

1611 Arrival of the Dutch traders.

1663–1664 The British establish trading posts on the Grain Coast; one of the posts is located at Mesurado but is later destroyed by the Dutch.

1700s Arrival of the first European traders, followed by Swedish traders.

February 6, 1820 Arrival of the first eighty-six freed slaves to the West African Coast, where they establish a settlement named Christopolis. The name is later changed to Monrovia in honor of James Monroe, a member of ACS and president of the United States. (Monroe was instrumental in the establishment of Liberia.) The 1820s mark the beginning of decades of immigration of freed slaves and the descendants of freed slaves from the United States and the Caribbean to the new colony.

December 1821 Cape Mesurado Colony was created by the American Society for Colonizing the Free People of Color in the United States (also known as the American Colonization Society or ACS).

August 1824 Cape Mesurado expands the settlement into the Colony of Liberia

1824 The US government settles New Georgia with Congos who were rescued. (These were African people from the Congo River Basin who had been captured for the slave market but then diverted to Liberia as slavery is abolished, without ever having been exposed to non-African cultures. In other words, they never made it to the Americas.)

April 1839 New Georgia is incorporated as the Commonwealth of Liberia, formally making the settlements of Liberia by the ACS and the US Government.

1841 Joseph Jenkins Roberts is appointed governor of the American Colonization Society (ACS), the first black man to serve.

July 26, 1847 The colony asserts its Declaration of Independence: the Republic of Liberia is officially established.

August 24, 1847 Liberian Flag Day: the initial unfurling and unveiling of the new Republic's flag, with one star in its blue field to represent the lone independent state in Africa, and eleven red and white stripes, representing the eleven signers of the Declaration.

1848 The United Kingdom and France are the first nations to recognize the independence of Liberia.

1848 The Liberian Constitution is ratified, and the first presidential elections were held, with Joseph Jenkins Roberts, a wealthy black merchant who had immigrated in 1829 from Petersburg, Virginia, elected president of the new Republic.

1856 War between the Grebo and Kru tribes leads the way for the last African American colony, the Republic of Mary of Maryland (now Maryland County), to join Liberia.

1857 The State of Maryland is incorporated into Liberia as Maryland County.

1862 Liberia's independence is formally recognized by the United States of America.

1862 Liberian borders officially established.

1864 An uprising of inland and coastal tribes occurs during the Steven Allen Benson presidency.

1875–1876 Another war in Cape Palmas, the capital of Maryland County. The incident happens during President James Spriggs Payne administration.

1886 A third uprising occurs during President Johnson's administration.

Between the 1880s and the 1890s some of the indigenous tribes are still at war with the settlement, taking place during the presidency of William D. Coleman.

1893 The Grebo tribe attacks the settlement at Harper when President Joseph James Cheeseman was in office.

1900 Another bloody battle between the settlement and the Grebo tribe, also during Cheeseman's presidency.

1912–1920 Rebellion of the Kru tribe against the settlement and an internal war happens, this time during the administration of President Daniel Edward Howard.

1917 Liberia declares war on Germany, giving the Allies a much-needed base in West Africa.

1919 Liberia signs as an original member of the League of Nations covenant after World War I.

1926 Firestone Tire and Rubber Company opens the world's largest rubber plantation on one million acres of land leased for a term of ninety-nine years from the Liberian government.

1930 The Christy Commission admonishes forced labor as a subset of slavery in existence in Liberia. Consequently, the United States and Britain break diplomatic relations with Liberia.

1936 Liberian government abolishes forced labor.

1944 Liberian government declares war on the Axis powers.

July 1948 A new era in trade relations between West Africa and the United States begin as the Republic of Liberia marks its 101st anniversary by formally opening its new $20,000,000 deep-water harbor to serve the capital city of Monrovia.

1951 Women and indigenous property owners vote in the presidential elections for the very first time.

February 1958 Liberian National Legislature approves new law making racial discrimination a crime punishable by a fine of up to $30,000 and jail terms in some cases.

August 10, 1958 Liberia officially bypasses the United States to become the world's top tanker power, a title it has held for almost twenty years, as reported in the *New York Times* Business Section.

1975 Liberia is a founding member of the Economic Community of West African States (ECOWAS)

1979 Rice Riots occur in Monrovia as a result of the increase in the price of imported rice.

April 12, 1980 A group of enlisted men led by Samuel K. Doe fight their way into the presidential mission and assassinate President William Tolbert. Shortly afterward, thirteen members of his cabinet are publicly executed.

1985 Former Army Commanding General Thomas Quiwonkpa invades Liberia by way of neighboring Sierra Leone and almost succeeds in toppling the government of President Samuel Doe. But members of the armed forces of Liberia repel Quiwonkpa's attack and execute him in Monrovia.

A new constitution establishes the second Republic of Liberia. President Samuel K. Doe, the 1980 leader, retains power as the head of state.

The National Patriotic Front of Liberia (NPFL), led by Charles Taylor, (a Doe associate), begins an uprising against the government, eventually toppling the administration of Samuel K. Doe. The coup leads to a destructive Civil War, in which various warlords and faction groups fight for control of the nation; the infrastructure of the country is almost totally destroyed.

1990 President Samuel K. Doe is captured by a group of rebels led by faction leader Prince Johnson. He is tortured and executed by members of Johnson's forces.

November 1990–March 1994 Amos Claudius Sawyer becomes Interim Leader for a transitional government.

1991 ECOWAS and the National Patriotic Front agree to disarm and set up an interim government.

1993 Another peace agreement between the National Patriotic Front and ECOWAS falls through and fighting resumes.

Chairman of Counsel of State;(meaning appointed not democratically elected)

March 1994–September 1994 David D. Kpomakor and Wilton Sankawulo

September 1994–August 1997 Ruth Sando Fahnbulleh Perry is appointed to serve as Liberia's and Africa's first female appointed head of state.

August 1996 Charles G. Taylor is elected president.

1999 A number of West African nations accuse Mr. Taylor of fueling the civil war in neighbor Sierra Leone.

2001 The United Nations Security Council re-imposes an arms embargo lifted earlier. The aim for the decision is to punish the Taylor administration for trading weapons for diamonds with Sierra Leonean rebels.

2002 More than fifty thousand Liberians and Sierra Leoneans flee fighting along the border between two nations. In February of that year, Charles Taylor declares a state of emergency.

2002 Charles Taylor lifts an eight month state of emergency and a ban on political parties after the treat from rebels decreased.

June 2003 Taylor is indicted by a UN-backed war-crime tribunal for his alleged role in backing rebels during the Sierra Leonean Civil War and for trading arms for diamonds. During that same year, peace talks in Ghana aimed at reaching a ceasefire begin. Rebels from the southern part of Liberia approach the capital city and fighting continues despite a ceasefire agreement.

August 11, 2003 President Charles Taylor leaves office and accepts political asylum in Nigeria.

August 2003–October 2003 Moses Zeh Blah serves as Interim Leader.

October 14, 2003 C. Gyude Bryant is appointed as Chairman of the Transition Government.

November 23 2005 After a first-round vote with sports celebrity candidate George Weah in the lead, run-off elections result in Ellen Johnson-Sirleaf becoming the first woman to be elected as an African head of state.

January 2006 Ellen Johnson-Sirleaf takes office as Liberia's first woman President.

February 2006 The Truth and Reconciliation Commission is set up to investigate human rights abuses before and during the Liberian Civil War waged 1979 through 2003.

Glossary of Key Terms

Abolish—to officially end a law or a system, as an abolishment of slavery.

Abolition—the art of abolishing or ending a system.

Accentuate—to make emphasis or to emphasize, to stress. Example, to accentuate the values and principles of the Civil Rights movement.

Accountability—the quality or state of being accountable (answerable); an obligation or willingness to accept responsibility or to account for one's actions, as in "public officials lacking accountability."

ACS—American Colonization Society, a quasi-philanthropic organization that helped established an African colony in West Africa in 1821.

African American—Americans of African descent.

Amalgamate—to mix, to come together, to join or blend; unite to form a bigger organization.

Amalgamation—the art of mixing or coming together as a unit.

Ambassador—an official envoy, especially a diplomatic agent of the highest rank accredited to a foreign government; an authorized representative or spokesperson of high rank for any entity.

Americo-Liberian—Liberians of American descent or descendents of freed American slaves.

Ancestor—a member of your family who lived in past times or a foregoing person (usually deceased) from whom one is descended.

Anthropologist—one who studies or specializes in the study of groups of people, their societies, beliefs, and ways of life.

Anthropology—the scientific study of groups of people—their society, beliefs, and ways of life.

Anti-Slavery—being opposed to or against slavery.

Assassinate—to murder a ruler or politician, usually for political reasons.

Assimilate—to accept someone completely as a member of a group, or to adapt to a group's culture in order to become an accepted member of a group.

Authoritarian—of, relating to, or favoring a concentration of power in a leader or an elite group not constitutionally responsible to the people.

Autocratic—having unlimited control over a group of people or country without regard to others' wishes or perspectives; as an autocratic government or style of leadership.

Bush School—a traditional educational system that teaches young men the African culture, values, and traditions before transitioning into adulthood.

Cold War—an unfriendly relationship between two countries that do not actually fight each other, particularly the period of tensions between the United States and the Soviet Union after World War II through 1990.

Collaborate—to work jointly with others or together, especially in intellectual endeavors.

Collaboration—the act of collaborating or working together.

Colonization—the act of colonizing a place or a country.

Colony—a country or an area that is ruled by another country. Up until 1846, Liberia was a colony of the American Colonization Society.

Commonwealth—a group of countries that are related politically or economically. For example, the group of independent countries that were once part of the British Empire but now associate freely are members of the Commonwealth of Great Britain.

Communism—a political system in which the government controls all the production of food and goods and there is no privately owned property.

Congo People—descendents of captured slaves from the Congo that were brought to Liberia at between 1822 and 1825 and the ensuing years.

Conspicuous—obvious to the eye or mind; attracting attention; striking.

Constitution—a set of laws and principles that describes the power and purpose of a particular government, organization, etc. For example, the Constitution of the Republic of Liberia or the US Constitution.

Constructive Engagement—the name given to American foreign doctrines of the Reagan Administration; especially the US policy toward the Apartheid system in South Africa in the early 1980s, promoted by an international anti-apartheid movement.

Coup d'etat—a sudden, decisive exercise of force in politics; especially, the violent overthrow or alteration of an existing government by a small group.

Creole—the culture, language, and people of mixed French and African descent, particularly those living in the West Indies (Haitian Creole). Creole is also spoken in Sierra Leone by descendents of free blacks that emigrated from England; but Creole is also spoken by the general public in Sierra Leone.

Delegate—one who acts or represents another or a group; to entrust or empower on behalf of another.

Delegation—a small group of people who are chosen to speak, vote, and make decisions for a larger group or organization.

Democracy—a system of government in which everyone in a country can vote to elect its leaders; a government by the people. The United States has a democratic system of government.

Descendent—someone who is related to a person who lived a long time ago. For example, most black Americans are descendants of African slaves.

Discriminate—to treat a person or group differently from another in an unfair way; to pick and choose based on a set of criteria, whether fair or unfair.

Dominant—strongest, most important, or most noticeable. Example, TV is the dominant source of information in our society.

Dominate—to have power or control over someone or something.

Emancipate—to free from restraint, control, or the power of another; esp. to free from bondage.

Emancipation—the act of setting one free from social, political, and legal rules.

Emigrate—to leave your own country in order to live in another.

Empire—a group of countries that are all controlled by one ruler or government.

Empirical—originating in or based on observation or experience.

Encompass—to form a circle around; enclose; to go completely around.

Entrepreneur—one who organizes, manages, and assumes the risk of a business or enterprise.

Grain Coast—the former name of what is present-day Liberia; a section of West Africa where Liberia is located.

Hougan—a Voodoo high priest.

Humanistic Capitalism—a concept that seeks to marry humanism, specifically the safety and health needs of people and the environment, with an embrace of market forces and a market economy. President Tolbert promoted this idea for the Liberian people during his administration.

Humanitarian—a person promoting human welfare and social reform, philanthropist.

Immigrant—someone who moves to another country, leaving his own.

Immigration—the process of entering another country in order to live there.

Independence—the freedom and ability to make your own decisions and take care of yourself without having to ask for help, permission, or money.

Indigenous—originating in a particular region, place or country; as in Native Americans.

Inspiration—something or someone that encourages you to do or produce something good. For example, Mr. Johnson was an inspiration for my work in Liberia.

Insurrection—rebellion, an attempt by a group of people within a country to take control using force or violence: *an armed insurrection led by the army.*

Longitudinal—dealing with the growth and change of individuals or groups over a period of years.

Malaria—a disease common in hot or tropical countries that is caused by a virus and spread by the bite of an infested mosquito.

Manumission—the act of freeing slaves, done at the will of the owner.

Manumitted—to let go; to release from slavery.

Maroon—A runaway slave in the West Indies who had banded together and subsisted independently with other runaways.

Massacre—to kill a lot of people, especially people who could not defend themselves.

Monopolize—assume complete possession or control of.

Monopoly—exclusive ownership through legal privilege, command of supply, or concerted action; exclusive possession or control.

Nationalism—loyalty and devotion to a nation, especially, a sense of national consciousness exalting one nation above all other and placing primary emphasis on promoting its culture and interest over those of other nations.

Native—one original country or land; a place where you and your ancestors were born: The Pope is visiting his native Poland.

Negotiate—to discuss something in order to reach an agreement. Example: the UN representatives are trying to negotiate a ceasefire.

Non-Alignment—not allied with any other nation or bloc; neutral.

Non-Alignment Movement or Non-Alliance Movement—an international organization of states considering themselves not formally aligned with or against any major power. As of 2010, the organization has 118 members and eighteen observer countries.

Open-Door Policy—the concept in foreign affairs that is welcoming to all others. As a theory, the *open-door policy* originates with British commercial practice. President Tubman promoted the policy in Liberia to encourage foreign investments.

Panoramic—an unobstructed or complete view of an area in every direction; comprehensive presentation of a subject.

Philanthropic—relating to philanthropy, the act of helping others.

Philanthropy—the practice of giving money and assistance to people who need it; benevolence.

Pilgrim—someone who travels a long way to a holy place for a religious reason.

Plantation—a large farm, especially in a hot country where a single crop such as sugar, tea, cotton, or rubber is grown: the Firestone Rubber Plantation in Liberia.

Poro Society—a secret African society formally practiced in Liberia to keep and pass knowledge and traditions through certain "rites of passage" to adulthood, intended for young men.

Rebellion—an organized attempt to change the government using violence; as in the case of the 1791 slaves revolt in Haiti.

Reparation—payment made to someone for damages or injuries that you have caused.

Repatriate—to send someone or something back to the country he, she, or it comes from.

Repatriation—the act of sending someone or something to its original home.

Revolt—a strong and often violent action against a government, a rule, law, etc.

Sande Society—a secret African society practiced formally in Liberia to keep and pass knowledge and traditions through certain "rites of passage" for adulthood; intended for young women.

Selective Engagement—principles of American foreign policy that chooses where and when to engage based on national-interest criteria. For example, the Bush Doctrine of selective engagement in the Middle East.

Settlement—an official agreement or decision that ends an argument. Also a small colony or newly established village, like the early settlements in the colony of Liberia

Settler—someone who sets up living conditions in a new place, usually where there are few people.

Social Construct—a concept or practice or socializing principle created by a particular group; a symbolic artifact.

Subjugate—to bring under control and governance as a subject; to conquer.

Transparency—free from pretense or deceit, openness; frank, easily detected or seen through, obvious, readily understood, clear.

Unambiguous—having or exhibiting a single, clearly defined meaning; without doubt or misunderstanding.

Yellow Fever—a fever caused by a virus passed by a mosquito bite, usually in the tropical part of the world. Example, many of the settlers died from yellow fever caused by a bite from mosquito in Liberia and Sierra Leone.

References

———. 1905. *West Africa Before Europe*. London: C.M. Philips.

———. 1908 *African Life and Customs*. London: C.M. Phillips.

———. (1967). *A Biography of President William V. S. Tubman*. London, England.

———. 1969. "Tribal Reaction to Nationalism," Part 1. *Liberian Studies Journal,* I(2), 1–22 (Greencastle).

———. 1970. "A Tribal Reaction to Nationalism," Part 3. *Liberian Studies Journal* II(2), 99–117. (Greencastle).

———. 1985. "Gola Resistance to Liberian 'Rule' in the Nineteenth Century, 1835—1905." *Liberia Forum,* I(1), 5–27. Bremen: Liberia Working Group.

———. 1989. *The Black Jacobins: Tousaaint L'Ouverture and the San Domingo Revolution.* Vintage, 2nd ed. Allison & Busby, London

———. 2000. "Optimality Theory, the Minimal-Word Constraint, and the Historical Sequencing of Substrate Influence in Pidgin/Creole Genesis," in John McWhorter. *Language Change and Language Contact in Pidgin and Creoles.* John Benjamins Publishing Company, Amsterdam. 335–354.

———— and John D. Garrigus. 2006. *Slave Revolution in the Caribbean, 1789–1804: A Brief History with Documents.* Bedford/St. Martin's Press. New York City, NY

————. *Civics for Liberian Schools.* New York: Collier-Macmillan International; 2nd edition (1966)

————. Jan. 14, 1883. "The Origin and Purpose of African Colonization: a Discourse Delivered at the 66th Anniversary of the American Colonization Society." Washington, DC.

————. Nov. 1867. "Liberia as a Means, Not an End." Liberian Independence Oration, July 26, 1867. African Repository, Washington, D.C.

————. Summer 1982. "Abraham Bishop, "The Rights of Black Men," and "Tthe American Reaction to the Haitian Revolution." *The Journal of Negro History* 67 (2): 148–154.

A. Doris Banks Henries. *Liberian Nation—A Short History.* New York. Herman Jaffe (1954)

Afro-American Almanac—African American History Resource. http://www.toptags.com/aama/events.acs.htm

Afro-American Almanac: The American Society for Colonizing the Free People of Color of the United States. http://www.toptaps.com/aama/events/acs.htminternational/spotlight/liberia/article2.htm.

Ajayi, J. F., and Ian Espie, Ian, eds. 1969., *A Thousand Years of West African History,* 2nd ed.) Abadan University Press, Nigeria, 1965.

Ajiriwe, Nnamdi. 1970. (1934). *Liberia in World Politics.* Greenwood Pub Group. Westport, CT. April 1970.

Akingbade, Harrison. "US Liberian Relations during World War II." Clark Atlanta University. Vol. 46, No. 1, 1st Qtr., 1985 pp. 25–36.

Akpan, Monday B. 1980. "The Practices of Indirect Rule in Liberia: The Laying of the Foundations. 1922–1915." In Eckhard Hinzen and Robert Kappel, eds. *Dependence, Underdevelopment and Persistent Conflict—On the Political Economy of Liberia.* Bremen. 57–168.

Alexander, Archibald. 1849. *A History of Colonization on the Western Coast of Africa.* Philadelphia, PA. Kessinger Publishing, LLC, pp.77–82, 2007.

American Colonization Society, The. http://webby.cc.denison.edu//~waite/liberia/history/acs.htm.

Anderson, Benjamin. 1971 (1870, 1912). *Journeys to Musadu.* London. Lithographic, Engraving Painting Co (1870)

Anderson, R. Earle, 1952. *Liberia: America's African Friend.* Chapel Hill.

Ani, Marimba. Evolution of an Africanist Perspective. Trento: Africa World press, (1994) http://www.columbia.edu/~hcb8/EWB_Museum/Evolution.html

Appy, Christian G. 2000. Cold War Constructions: The Political Culture of United States Imperialism. University of Massachusetts Press.

Bellman, Beryl. 1975. *Village of Curers and Assassins.* The Hague: Mouton.

Birney, James G., Liberian Colonization (Examination of the decision of the Supreme Court of the United States, in the case of Strader, Gorman, and Armstrong versus Christopher Graham, delivered at its December term, 1850: concluding with an address to the free colored people, advising them to remove to Liberia/ by James G. Birney. Cornell University Library, Ithaca, NY (1857).

Blackburn, Robin. 2006. "Haiti, Slavery, and the Age of the Democratic Revolution." *William and Mary Quarterly* 63.4, 633–674.

Blackpast.org. Haitian Revolution 1791–1804.

Bledsos, Caroline H. 1980. *Women and Marriage in Kpelle Society.* Stanford.

Bloomington, IN (2005).

Blyden, E.W. "The Negro in Ancient History, Liberia: Past Present, and Future." *Methodist Quarterly Review. 2008*

Boley, George E. Saigbe. 1983. *Liberia—The Rise and Fall of the First Republic.* London.

Boone, C.C. 1970 (1929). *Liberia as I Know It.* Westport.

Brehun, Leonard. 1991. *Liberia: The War of Horror.* Adwinsa Publications

Brinton, Lauren, and Leslie Arnovick. 2006. *The English Language: A Linguistic History.* Canada: Oxford University Press. London, England

Carey, Mathew. "Formation of the ACS 1760–1839." http://ourworld. cs.com/ceoofamcolso/id5.hml.

Carter, P. III, *US Policy in Africa in the Twenty-First Century,* Bureau of African Affairs, Washington DC (2009)

Cassell, C. Abayomi, *Liberia: The History of the African republic;* New York: Fountainhead Publishers Inc, 1970.

Censer, Jack and Lynn Hunt. 2001. *Library, Equality, Fraternity: Exploring the French Revolution.* University Park, PA: Pennsylvanian State University Press.

Conclusion of the Special Commissioner on the Grievances pro and con of the Americo-Liberian and Aboriginal Liberians of Maryland County, Harper, August 11, 1875, in: Abasiattai, M. B.: "Resistance of the African People of Liberia." Liberia-Forum, 3/4, Bremen 1987, 60

Cooper, John Milton. 2009. Woodrow Wilson. Chs. 20–22 d'Azevedo, Warren L. 1969. "A Tribal Reaction to Nationalism," Part 2. *Liberian Studies Journal,* II(1), 43–65

Davenport, Frances Gardiner, ed. *European Treaties Bearing on the History of the United States, and Its Dependencies to 1648.* Carnegie Institution of Washington, DC. The Bull Inter Caetera (Alexander VI), May 4, 1492. http://www.nativeweb.org/pages/legal.indig-inter-caetera.html.

Davidson, Basil. 1981. *A History of West Africa 1000–1800*: Langman Group Ltd. 65, 78–96.

Dempster, Roland T. 2009. Sea Breeze Journal of Comtemorary Liberian Writings

Dubois, Laurent. 2005. *Avengers of the New World: The Story of the Haitian Revolution.* Cambridge, MA: Belknap Press of Harvard University.

Dunn, Elwood D., and Svend E Holsoe. 1985. *Historical Dictionary of Liberia.* African Historical Dictionaries Series. Metuchen: Scarecrow Press.

Dunn, Elwood D. *Liberia and the United States during the Cold War: Limits of Reciprocity,* Palgrave Macmillan; New York, NY (2009)

Elliot, Charles Wyllys. 1905. "The Negro Revolution in Haiti: Toussaint Louverture Establishes the Dominion of His Race." *The Great Events by Famous Historians.*

Elliot, C. W. 1855. St. Domingo: Its Revolutions and Its Hero, Toussant Louverture. New York: J. A. Dix.

Eric Burin. September 2006. *The Journal of American History.* Bloomington: 93(2), 517–518.

Garrigus, John D. 2006. *Before Haiti: Race and Citizenship in Saint-Domingue (Americas in the Early Modern Atlantic World)*. Palgrave-Macmillan.

Geggus, David P. 2002. *Haitian Revolutionary Studies*. University of South Carolina Press. Columbia, South Carolina

Greenleaf, Simon. "Testimony of the Evangelists." http://www.myfortress.org/simongreenleaf.html.

Hall, Richard L. *On Afric's Shore: A History of Maryland in Liberia, 1834–1857*. Maryland Historical Society. (2003).

History of Liberia: A time line. http://memory.loc.gov/gmmem/gmdhtml/liberia.

Huberich, Charles Henry. 1947. *The Political and Legislative History of Liberia*. New York: Central Book Co., 1947. 1:145.

Huffman, Alan. June 2009. "Tumult and Transition in '"Little America." *Smithsonian Magazine* pp. 46–53.

Hull, Cordell. (2008) *The Memoirs Of Cordell Hull*. Vol. 11. Thornhill, Ontaio Reprint Services Corp.

Hyman, Lester S., *United States Policy Towards Liberia, 1822 to 2003: Unintended Consequences;* Africana Homestead Legacy Publishers, Cherry Hill, NJ (2010).

James, C.L.R. 1980. *The Black Jacobins: Toussaint L'Ouverture and the San Domingo Revolution*. 1928, 2nd ed. London: Allison & Busby. vii.

Kelvin Alfred Strom. American Dissident Voices—Forbidden Truths Today. National Alliance, Hillsboro, (1993)http://www.natvan.com/american-dissident-voices/adv022093.html.

Kraaij, Fred P.M. van der. 1983. "The Open Door Policy of Liberia. An Economic history of Modern Liberia, In *The Origins of the Closed Door Policies and Open Door Policies 1847–1947.* Bremen. 12–46.

Kramer, Reed. A Casualty of the Cold War's End. CSIS Africa Notes, Washington, D C 1995.

Kremer, Gary R. 1991. *James Milton Turner and the Promise of America.* University of Missouri Press. Columbia

Liberia, Africa, History. http://mo.essortment.com/liberiahistory/acs.htm.

"Liberia: America's Impoverished Orphan in Africa" *Washington Post.* http://www.media.washingtonpost.com/wp-adv/specialsales/international/spotlight/liberia/article2htm

———. *Liberia's Fulfillment: Achievements of the Republic of Liberia during twenty-five years under the administration of President William V. S. Tubman 1944–1969.* Monrovia, 1969

Manela, Erez. 2007. *The Wilsonian Moment: Self-Determination and the International Origins of Anticolonial Nationalism (Oxford Studies in International History).* Oxford University Press, USA; 1 edition (January 9, 2009)

Mathewson, Tim. Mar. 1996. "Jefferson and the Nonrecognition of Haiti." *Proceeding of the American Philosophical Society* 140 (1): 22–48.

McPherson, J.H.T., *The History of Liberia, Seattle,* WA: Kessinger Publishing, May 2010

Moore, Bai T. (1968). *Murder in the Cassava Patch.* Ducor Publishing, Monrovia-Liberia.

Moses, Wilson J. *Liberian Dreams: Back –To-Africa Narratives from the 1850s;* Pennsylvania State University Press, University Park, PA (1998).

Nelson, Harold D. ed, *Liberia: a Country Study,* Washington DC; US Government Printing Office 1985

Page, Ann Randolph. The American Colonization Society. http:www.vts. edu/logue/AnnRPage/liberia.htm.

Reef, Catherine, *This Our Dark Country: The American Settlers of Liberia;* Clarion Books, New York, NY 92002).

Schick, Tom W. 1980. *Behold the Promised Land: A History of Afro-American Settlers in Nineteenth-Century Liberia (Johns Hopkins Studies in Atlantic History and Culture).* Baltimore: Johns Hopkins University Press.

Schwarz, Benjamin. March 1997. "What [Thomas] Jefferson Helps to Explain." *The Atlantic Monthly.* 279.

Sherwood, Henry Noble. 1882. "The Formation of the American Colonization Society." *Negro History* 2(3) July 1917. 209–228. http:docsouth.unc.edu/church/sherwood/sherwood.html

Shick, Tom W. "Roll of Emigrants to Liberia, 1820–1843 and Liberian Census Data, 1843." University of Wisconsin, Madison. http://www. disc.edu/Liberia/. Retrieved on 2008. 12–12.

Singler, John Victor. 1986. "Copula Variation in Liberian Settler English and American Black English," in Geneva Smitherman. ed. *Talkin and Testifyin: The Language of Black America,* Wayne State University Press, Detroit. 129–164.

Smith. Jeff Kooper. "Liberian Revisionist History." *American Politics Journal.* http://www.americanpolitics.com/2003078koop.html.

Smith, Liberian Revisionist History. http://www.youtube.com/ watch?v=—ps4XtDryIww.

Stanley, William R. August 1994. "Trans-South Atlantic Air Link in World War II," *Heo Journal* 33(4).

Staudenraus, P.J. 1980 (1961). *The African Colonization Movement, 1816–1865.* New York: Columbia University Press. New York: Octagon Books.

Tellewoyan, Joseph. "Bird's-Eye View of Liberian History and Government." http://www.africawithin.com/liberia/hist_gov.htm. ———.

The Constitution of the American Society, for Colonizing the Free People of Color of the United States. http://www.toptags.com/aama/docs/acscon.htm.

The Constitution of the Commonwealth of Liberia. 1839. http://www.toptags.com/aama/docs/liberia.con.htm.

The Constitution of the United States. 1787. http://www.house.gov/constitution/constitution.html.

Tyson, George F., Tyson, ed., 1971. *Toussaint L'Oouverture: Great Lives Observed* Series Englewood Cliffs: Prentice Hall, Inc. (6).

Unger, Sanford J., and Vale Peter. (1985). "South Africa: Why Constructive Engagement Failed," *Foreign Affairs,* 64(2):234–58.

US Constitution, Article II, Section 2. http://www.archives.gov/national-archives-experience/charters/constitution.html.

US Government Printing Office. 1931. "Report of the International Commission of Inquiry into The the Existence of Slavery and Forced Labor in the Republic of Liberia." Washington, DC.

van der Kraaij, Fred P.M. 1983. "The Open Door Policy of Liberia. An Economic History of Modern Liberia," ch. 2. Bremen.

Van der Kraaij, Fred P.M. (1983). "The Origins of the Closed Door Policies and Open Door Policies 1847–1947." 12–46. Bremen.

Verlag, Horst Erdmann. 1970. *Liberian Writing, Liberia as Seen by Her Own Writers as well as by German Authors.* Tübingen.

Weisberger, B. Dec. 1995. "America's African Colony." *American Heritage,* 46(8), 26. Retrieved June 3, 2009, from EBSCO MegaFile database.

Whitton, John B. (Jan. 1951). "Cold War Propaganda" *The American Journal of International Law,* 45:1, 151–153.

Woahtee, J., *America and Liberia: a Mother/Stepchild Relationship Betrayed,* AuthorHouse, Bloomington, IN (2005).

Wulah, Teah; *The Forgotten Liberian: History of Indigenous Tribes,* Authorhouse, Bloomington, IN (2005).

Yarema, Allan E. American Colonization Society. University Press of America, (2006) http://voyager.dvc.edu/~mpowell/afam/ps_ACS. htm Accessed